CASE STUDIES IN
CULTURAL ANTHROPOLOGY

GENERAL EDITORS

George and Louise Spindler

STANFORD UNIVERSITY

THE CHEYENNES
Indians of the Great Plains

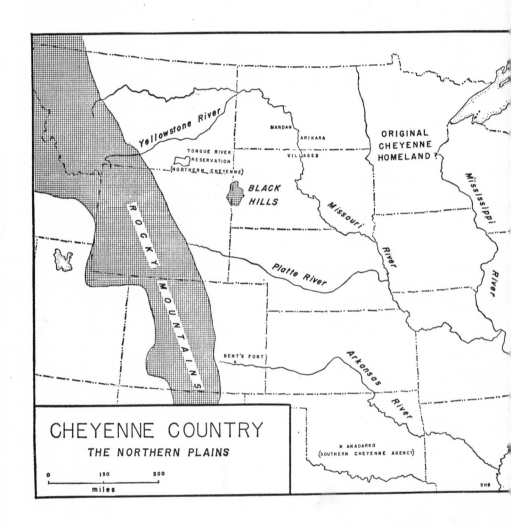

Yellowstone River

MANDAN
ARIKARA
VILLAGES

ORIGINAL
CHEYENNE
HOMELAND ?

TONGUE RIVER
RESERVATION
(NORTHERN CHEYENNE)

BLACK
HILLS

R O C K Y   M O U N T A I N S

Missouri River

Mississippi River

Platte River

BENT'S FORT

Arkansas River

CHEYENNE COUNTRY
THE NORTHERN PLAINS

0   150   300
miles

X ANADARKO
(SOUTHERN CHEYENNE AGENCY)

SHB

THE

CHEYENNES

Indians of the Great Plains

BY

E. ADAMSON HOEBEL

University of Minnesota

HOLT, RINEHART AND WINSTON
New York • Chicago • San Francisco
Toronto • London

To my father and mother

About the Author

E. ADAMSON HOEBEL is professor of anthropology at the University of Minnesota. He holds the Ph.D. in anthropology from Columbia. For a number of years he taught anthropology at New York University and subsequently at the University of Utah, where he was also Dean of the University College (Arts and Sciences). He has done fieldwork among the Northern Cheyenne (1935 and 1936) and among the Comanches (1933), Northern Shoshone (1934), and Pueblo Indians of New Mexico (1945-1949). He is the author of *Man in the Primitive World, The Political Organization and Law-ways of the Comanche Indians,* and *The Law of Primitive Man.* He is coauthor (with K. N. Llewellyn) of *The Cheyenne Way* and (with Ernest Wallace) of *The Comanches.* Dr. Hoebel is a past-president of the American Ethnological Society and the American Anthropological Association, and is a director of the Social Science Research Council and member of the Advisory Panel, Office of Social Science Research, National Science Foundation.

About the Book

This is a lively book about a high-spirited but self-controlled people who had a complex, satisfying way of life before it was uprooted by the white man. With the help of the Cheyenne elders still living when he did his fieldwork, and through a masterly study of the surviving culture, Dr. Hoebel has made this way of life live again.

A well-rounded picture of the Cheyenne emerges in this case study. They are a people who are not "typical" of anything—the Cheyenne are too unique for that—but they represent much of the Plains Indian way of life that is so much a part of the drama of our West.

Among the people with whom Dr. Hoebel has worked the Cheyenne stand out as a group who have won his admiration and liking. Their democratic tolerance; the value they place upon individual liberty, balanced by group cooperativeness; their intellectual stamina, balanced with activity; their self-assurance—all of these qualities place the Cheyenne high on a scale of values that we can all appreciate. But the Cheyenne created and maintained these values within a framework of social life very different from our own. A case study of the Cheyenne therefore offers the opportunity of gaining a new perspective on human behavior.

GEORGE AND LOUISE SPINDLER
General Editors

Stanford, California
December 1959

Contents

Wolf Robe, born 1841. Photo by De Lancey Gill, B.A.E., 1909. (Courtesy the Smithsonian Institution, Bureau of American Ethnology)

Spirit Woman, born 1858. Photo by De Lancey Gill, B.A.E., 1908. (Courtesy the Smithsonian Institution, Bureau of American Ethnology)

A Cheyenne camp. From a photograph by William S. Soulé, 1867-74.
(Courtesy the Smithsonian Institution, Bureau of American Ethnology)

Cheyenne warriors.

Introduction

THE CHEYENNE INDIANS, or *Tsistsistas,* meaning "The People," are one of the most notable of the western tribes who inhabited the Great Plains, the open country lying west of the Mississippi River and east of the Rocky Mountains. They were famous among early travelers for the chastity of their women and the courage of their warriors; in later years, when everything was in change, they were considered the most conservative of the Plains Indians. Their attitudes toward sex and war, and toward the maintenance of their social order are the outstanding features of their way of life. These will be the main themes in the study of this culture. Our case study will undertake to analyze the reasons for the Cheyenne attitudes; it will show how these attitudes produced a distinctive effect on Cheyenne behavior, and how the Cheyennes worked out a remarkably effective and satisfying society. Our major concern will be to show how prior and present social history, basic cultural premises, psychological traits, physical and biological environment, and social structure all interact to give a culture its characteristic cast.

Several hundred years ago, the Cheyennes resided in the woodland country of the western Great Lakes (probably in the vicinity of Lake Superior). Toward the end of the seventeenth century they migrated westward, settling on the Red River where it forms the border between Minnesota and the Dakotas. Early in the eighteenth century they became closely associated with the sedentary village tribes of the upper Missouri River—namely, the Mandan, Hidatsa, and Arikara. These tribes were old-time gardeners who relied upon hunting for subsidiary subsistence. They lived in permanent villages constructed of large, semisubterranean earth lodges (see Wilson 1934). They were organized into matrilineal clans, and a married couple lived with the bride's parents. During the eighteenth century, and for the first decade or two of the nineteenth, the Cheyennes settled down in earth lodge villages and grew corn, beans, and squash in the manner of their new neighbors. Their way of life was both sedate and sedentary. Then came the introduction of the horse (ca. 1760),

1

and new vistas opened for the Cheyenne. The plains were teeming with bison, an extremely rich source of food and derivative by-products, if only one could conveniently traverse the great dry stretches between the widely scattered waterways with reasonable prospects of locating the herds, and with the means to transport enough meat to the base camp to sustain the tribe through the winter. Where men on foot found such prospects dim, men on horseback found them bright. By 1830, the Cheyennes were sufficiently equipped with horses to have completely abandoned the village life of gardeners for the nomadic life of hunters. Simultaneously, they were adding guns to their hunting and fighting equipage. Mobility and the great prizes to be won in hunt and war transformed much of their culture, but the past—as always—left its imprint.

The Cheyennes, as they are to be presented in this case study, are the Cheyennes of the period 1840-60, when their adaptation to nomadic horse culture was at flood tide, when white hunters had not yet exterminated the buffalo, nor had settlers preempted their lands, nor had the United States military beaten them into submission. This book is therefore written in the "ethnographic present," which means that it is presented descriptively in the present tense, although in fact things are not today, and have not been for some time, as described. The reader should keep this in mind.

From 1857 to 1879 the Cheyennes were embroiled in almost continuous fighting with the Americans. The wars were not of their own choosing, but were forced upon them by whites who were little disposed to discriminate among Indians. The Cheyennes were made to suffer for the more aggressive hostility of Sioux, Kiowas, and Comanches, until they, too, were inextricably involved in the bitter, bloody death-struggles from which there was no escape but humiliating surrender and the ignoble lassitude of reservation life. A number of the fights were pitched battles between campaigning troops and sizable bodies of warriors; some, such as those at Ash Hollow (1855) and Sand Creek (1864), were unprovoked assaults on friendly Cheyenne camps in which women and children were slaughtered along with the men who tried to defend them. The Cheyennes played a large part in the repulse of Custer's attack on the Cheyenne-Sioux encampment on the Little Big Horn (1876) when Custer and his command were annihilated. In spite of their successes at the Custer fight, and the defeats inflicted on Crook and others of his predecessors, the Cheyennes succumbed after the final destruction of the camps of Dull Knife and Two Moons, in 1877 and 1878.

The Northern Cheyennes were herded south and confined with the Southern Cheyennes in what is now Oklahoma. Disease and malnutrition, for they were not used to the hot lower-lying lands, decimated their numbers and brought them to the point of hopeless desperation. In the summer of 1878, under the leadership of the wise Dull Knife (Morning Star) and the redoubtable Little Wolf, three hundred Northern Cheyennes—men, women, and children—defied the Indian Agent and the United States Army by starting the long march home. "Never was such a journey since the Greeks marched to the sea." Thirteen thousand troops tried to stay them. They fought and marched, fought and marched, until they reached their beloved homeland, whereupon they laid down their arms. Obdurate officialdom in Washington ordered them to return under armed escort in dead winter to the Oklahoma from which they had escaped and in doing so sacrificed so much. Confined in unheated barracks, without food or water for days (an effort by the authorities to break their stubborn refusal to give in), they at last broke out to meet death on the night of January 9, 1879. Sixty-four were killed by the troops and seventy-eight were recaptured. Thirty or so escaped.

Separate reservations were established shortly after on the Tongue River, in Montana, and in southwestern Oklahoma. In the north, the Cheyennes now subsist mostly as cattle raisers. In Oklahoma they do small farming. In the mid-1930's each unit elected to take on modern forms of tribal business organization under the Indian Reorganization Act. The Sun Dance is still an annual affair, but the Peyote Cult has become the major form of religious expression for most Cheyennes; Christianity for some.

The materials on which this book is based were mostly derived from the Northern Cheyennes, those who, in the period of the study, lived in what is now western Montana, eastern Wyoming, and northwestern Nebraska. The Southern Cheyennes are those bands which, after 1833, stayed for the most part in southern Colorado, to be near the famous trading post established by Charles and William Bent on the Arkansas River in southeastern Colorado (Lavender 1954). Both the Northern and Southern Cheyennes retained their unity as a single tribe, however, and they are treated as such in this discussion.

The author did extensive field work among the Northern Cheyennes in 1935 and 1936. Old people were still living then who had vivid and well-informed memories of the old days. Fortunately, the Northern Cheyennes were intensively studied at first hand from about 1885 to 1910 by a very acute and sympathetic observer, George Bird Grinnell, whose two-volume work, *The Cheyenne Indians,* is a classic of anthropological research. It was my good fortune to be aided throughout my own Cheyenne field studies by Mr. Grinnell's old interpreter and friend, High Forehead (Willis Rowland). I also had the unstinting friendship and cooperation of a number of elderly Cheyennes. It is on the basis of what I learned from them and the researches of Grinnell that this book primarily rests. It also draws to a lesser extent upon the Cheyenne studies of Fred Eggan, James Mooney, and George A. Dorsey, in particular; and it has been influenced by Thomas Gladwin's brief but provocative article on Cheyenne and Comanche personality. Their works, and those of others, are indicated in the bibliography.

PART ONE

Ritual and Tribal Integration

The Great Ceremonies

The Arrow Renewal

A T THE TIME of the Renewal of the Sacred Arrows the summer sun is at its highest; its rising is farthest north on the eastern horizon; its position at noon is as close to the zenith as it can come. Spring has run its course; it is roughly the time of the summer solstice. The life-giving forces have waxed to their fullest strength.

On a broad, yet sheltered, flat near a good stream of water, where there is plenty of forage for the horse herds, the entire Cheyenne tribe gathers to renew its vitality. Eight hundred to a thousand tipis are raised in a great open circle, in the form of the new moon. They form a broad crescent with the gap between the horns facing the northeast, the point of the rising sun. The entrance of each family tipi also faces east, so that the sun's first rays will shine into the lodge. In the clear, open space of the great camp circle stand three isolated tipis. In the center is a huge, conical skin lodge, the Sacred Arrow Lodge. Off to the right is the lodge of the Sacred Arrow Keeper. At the edge of the open space, behind the Sacred Arrow Lodge, is the Offering Lodge, which is the tipi of the pledger of the ceremony.

In the great circle of family tipis, the lodges are grouped by bands. Each of the ten bands of the Cheyennes camps together as a unit within the whole. Throughout the long winter, the bands, and even the family groups within the bands, have been scattered in smaller camps hidden in cottonwood groves along the watercourses, many miles apart. When spring was once more upon the land, an enterprising Cheyenne had made the rounds of all the camps. Sometime during the previous year, he had assumed the responsibility of organizing the Medicine (or Sacred) Arrow Renewal Rite. He had made a pledge or vow to the supernatural forces to do this thing. His kinsmen had helped him accumulate the necessary food and gifts. He had taken his ceremonial pipe and sufficient tobacco. He had traveled across the plains, seeking out every

6

Cheyenne encampment, convening with the camp chiefs, offering them his pipe, and telling them of the place where the Arrow Renewal would be held.

Through the first weeks of summer, the bands had been steadily moving in toward the rendezvous, as if drawn by strands of invisible thread radiating out from a single center. Each band had stopped four times on its journey to pray and, in solemn ceremony, to smoke to the four directions and to the Great Medicine Spirits above. On the day before arriving at the appointed place, they had halted to don their finest clothing. Scouts from the main camp, where the pledger's people had been getting everything in readiness, had reported their approach. Now, their horses groomed and painted, themselves in full paint and finery, they had approached the spot of the camp circle from the east, riding in a long column, singing songs of happiness. All those who had reached the camp ahead of them had turned out in force to cheer and applaud them as they paraded around the camp circle and then went to the section of the arc traditionally reserved for them. Their women had quickly unloaded the pack horses; soon their lodges had been raised, and the cooking fires started. Invitations to meals had been sent back and forth, and friends and relatives had had a busy round of visiting, gossiping, eating, and gambling.

Now, however, not a sound may be heard in the camp, save the murmur of voices of the priests in the Medicine Arrow Lodge, or of the ceremonial drumming and singing that comes through the skins of the lodge. No one is to be seen, except the members of a warrior society silently pacing the rounds of the camp. An occasional man may emerge from his tipi quietly to go out on a necessary task. Women and children remain silent behind the closed coverings of the lodges. Even the dogs skulk without a sound. Should one so much as growl or yelp, his skull is shattered with a swift blow of a patrolling warrior's club. In the great lodge, the priests have opened the fox-skin bundle in which the four Sacred Arrows are kept. It is the moment of supreme sacredness of the Cheyenne as a people. It is the moment at which the well-being of the tribe as a whole is in the process of renewal. The ordinary individual is but a minute particle that must suspend its activities in the solemnity of an activity that focuses on the life of the society.

The Medicine Arrows symbolize the collective existence of the tribe. In a sense, they may be called the embodiment of the tribal soul. As the Arrows prosper, the tribe prospers; as they are allowed to suffer neglect, the tribe declines in prosperity. Their attributes are not in their material form, but in their ineffable supernatural qualities. Or in another sense, they may properly be called the supreme tribal fetish, a set of objects in which resides a spiritual power that belongs to all the people and is revered by all. The Arrows were given to the Cheyennes by their mythological culture hero, Sweet Medicine (*Mutsoyef*), who is believed to have brought to the Cheyennes many of their ways. He had been a strange and handsome youth with mysterious habits. As a married man, in his early maturity, he had journeyed with his wife to the Sacred Mountain by the Black Hills. There, in a great cave, he had sat with the selected wise men of all the peoples of the earth as a pupil to Maiyun (the personified great spirit). Maiyun gave four arrows to Sweet Medicine and instructed him in their care and use. Two of these arrows have power over buffalo and two have power over human beings. When the buffalo Arrows are ritually pointed toward animals, they become confused and helpless, are easily surrounded and killed. When the Arrows are carried against an enemy tribe on the rare occasions when the Cheyenne go on the warpath with all the tribe along, the man Arrows are ritually pointed at the enemy before the attack. The foe becomes blinded and befuddled. Thus, the Arrows are the Cheyennes' greatest resource against their most besetting manifest anxieties: failure of the food supply and extermination by enemies. The Arrows, as the supernaturals' great gift to the Cheyennes, are their central insurance for survival. For all their consummate skill as hunters and warriors, they know full well they cannot succeed all the time. In spite of their best efforts, starvation haunts them. In spite of their wily skill at arms, their braves are turned back defeated, their camps surprised, their horses run off, their people slain, scalped, or led off into captivity. The Arrows are proof against ultimate disaster, an assurance that in spite of everything all *will* prosper.

Of the solemn ritual of the Renewal of the Arrows only the barest outline is known. The Cheyennes who have described the ceremony are not themselves priests of the Sacred Arrows and only these priests know what goes on in the great lodge when the Arrows are unwrapped. But what they have described is in essence the following.

The Sacred Arrow Renewal is not an annual ceremony. In off years, either the Sun Dance or the Animal Dance (Massaum) will be performed in its stead. The Arrow Renewal Rite is pledged by an individual who wishes to do a great thing. It is a commitment to the supernaturals, undertaken as a vow under great stress or anxiety. A man who hopes for the recovery of a close kinsman, a brother, son, or wife, may promise to sponsor a Renewal. A man who is himself deathly sick may vow to do it if he survives. A warrior in mortal danger may be the one to vow to undertake it. These are voluntary acts, but done always under the duress of threatened personal loss. Under one circumstance, which we will elaborate later on, it is absolutely imperative that a Renewal be pledged and performed as soon as possible. This is when one Cheyenne has killed another. Murder within the tribe is the most horrendous of crimes and sins. Not only does the murderer become internally polluted and begin to rot inside, but flecks of blood soil the feathers of the Arrows. Bad luck dogs the tribe, and all game shun its territory until atonement is made in the Renewal and clean feathers replace those that are sullied on the Arrows. These are the ostensible reasons for holding the ceremony, which lasts four days.

The first day is given over to the making of offerings and preparing the sacred Arrow Lodge. The Offering Lodge belongs to the pledger and is raised by his wife. People bring what they wish to give to Maiyun. These items are hung together on a pole in front of the lodge, or over its door. Early in the afternoon, all the warriors gather to select the spot for the Sacred Arrow Lodge. This done, they choose from among their number enough men of unspotted reputations to go out and cut a supply of extra-large lodge poles.

The next job is to get a covering. The warriors appoint a delegation to visit two men who have been brave in war, generous, good, and even-tempered throughout their lives. These exemplars of Cheyenne virtue are singled out and honored with a request for the loan of the covers of their tipis to use on the Sacred Arrow Lodge. When the huge lodge has been raised and covered, the Arrow Keeper and his associated priests enter it, strip off the sod, and smooth out the ground. They prepare a hearth in the center and a ceremonial sand altar (a mound) near the rear of the tipi. Sage, which is always a ceremonial purifier, is laid around the outer edges of the space; upon it the medicine men will sit.

On the second morning, the priests take their places in the Sacred Arrow Lodge. The pledger of the ceremony, naked except for a buffalo robe, his body painted red, leads three other good men to the Offering Lodge. The sacrificial gifts are removed from their position and carried single file into the Sacred Arrow Lodge, where they are placed as an offering before the altar. The four men then leave the lodge, walking slowly in the direction of the Sacred Arrow Keeper's tipi, wailing and keening as they go. Before the tipi door they advance and retreat four times before entering. The Arrow Keeper awaits them. They sit. He prays for them. The Arrow Bundle is then placed in their custody. In single file before the Keeper's tipi, they pray again as the pledger holds the bundle on his left arm. Slowly, very slowly, they move off in the direction of the Renewal Lodge. The mystic number four is observed again, as they halt four times on their traverse. In the lodge, the bundle is placed by the head priest on a prepared bed behind the altar. The ceremony proper is ready to begin; the warrior patrols begin their rounds of the camp, and we are now at the point at which we came upon the camp in the opening of this description.

Within the Renewal Lodge the secret rituals preparatory to the opening of the bundle are begun. At last, with great care, the bundle is unwrapped and the Arrows exposed and examined. If the feathers are not in perfect condition, a man who has lived in accordance with Cheyenne ideals is appointed to undertake the great task. He must be healthy, clean, good tempered, kind, generous, wise, and brave, never guilty of a dishonorable act. The work of renewal is performed on the third day.

The main performance of the third day symbolizes the unity of all the individual Cheyenne families in the one great entity—the tribe. A willow tally stick a yard long is prepared for every living Cheyenne family, save those who have produced a murderer. The counting sticks are laid in a pile beside the altar. In front, and to the side of the main fireplace, are two small incense fires that are kept aglow throughout the entire ceremony. One by one, the family counting sticks are smoked in the incense to bless every family individually and to give it well-being. During this part of the ceremony, all the medicine men in the camp are going through their private rituals of renewing the supernatural power of their medicine paraphernalia.

On the fourth and final day, the Arrows are exposed to the sun, and to public view. The pledger of the ceremony obtains a forked pole which he ritually carries into the Arrow Lodge. There the high priest affixes the Arrows to the pole. Wailing as he slowly walks from the lodge to a point some distance in front of the door, the pledger carries the pole and Arrows into the open. After he has returned to the lodge for the skin wrapper, which is placed on the ground before the pole, the priests bring forth the offerings that have been resting in the lodge. Boys bring additional offerings from their homes to place alongside the pole, as. well. Now, while all the women are securely hidden in their tipis, every Cheyenne male, from the smallest babe in arms to the oldest dodderer, passes before the Arrows to receive their beneficent effect. They may look at the Arrows, but they are hard to see, for they give off a shining, blinding light. When all the males have passed before the Arrows, the warriors dismantle the Sacred Arrow Lodge, which is then set up over the Arrows and the offerings where they stand. This time, however, a third tipi cover is added to the original two, so that a lodge large enough to crowd in all the medicine men of the tribe is formed. The new lodge is called Sweet Medicine's Lodge, the home of the culture hero himself. The Sacred Arrows are now removed from this lodge and returned to the tipi of their regular keeper. In the meantime, a sweat-bath lodge is erected on the spot where the Offering Tipi had stood.

On the fourth and final night, the head chief of all the Cheyennes, who is himself called the Sweet Medicine Chief and thus represents the culture hero, enters the Sweet Medicine Lodge, followed by all the medicine men. They solemnly sing the four sacred songs that Maiyun had taught Sweet Medicine in the sacred mountain. After each song, they prophesy the future of the Cheyennes, even as Sweet Medicine had done when he returned to the tribe after his stay in the mountain. At long last, just before daybreak, all the participants repair to the sweat lodge for a steam bath which ritually decontaminates them, so that they may resume ordinary living and go among the women and children without danger. When the bath is finished, it is the dawn of the fifth day. After four days of confinement, the women may throw back the door coverings of their tipis and emerge into the open. Life is renewed, purified, and strengthened because it has been resanctified. Now the great communal hunts may follow.

A great tribal undertaking such as this has a number of aspects and effects:

1. It emphasizes the dependence of human beings (the Cheyennes) upon the beneficent help of the supernatural world. It reinforces the assumption that all that is good and desirable comes from the mystic beings.

2. It restates the norms of right conduct in individual and group life as formulated by Sweet Medicine in the long ago. The prophecies tell how the Cheyennes will prosper, if they act in the right way, and what will befall them, if they do not. To the sacred authority of tribal custom it adds the sanctity of ancient origin. It also singles out for signal honor men who are neither chiefs nor priests but whose lives have conformed to the ideal.

3. It guarantees the authority of the tribal chiefs, especially of the head chief, who, by virtue of his possession of the sweet medicine bundle given to

the tribe by Sweet Medicine himself, is the living incarnation of the long-dead creator of the Cheyenne way, Sweet Medicine.

4. It reinforces the authority of the old men of the tribe in general and all medicine men in particular.

5. It stamps the domination of males over females in ultimate determination of tribal matters, since men alone may actively participate in the rite.

6. Finally, and above all, it functions as the great symbolic integrator of the tribe, ritually demonstrating that the tribe, although its group components are the kindred (represented by the counting sticks), is more than the sum of its parts and that the parts must not act in a way that will sever the whole. (Separatistic and disruptive tendencies in Cheyenne life will be discussed later.) In a more pragmatic and less symbolic manner, this concept is sustained in another way in the great communal buffalo hunt upon which the Cheyennes launch themselves as soon as the ritual is over.

The Sun Dance

The Sacred Arrows and the rite of their renewal are unique to the Cheyennes. Not so the Sun Dance, which is a ceremony common to most Plains Indian and a few Great Basin tribes (see Spier 1921). The central features of the Sun Dance are the same among all tribes, but there are many differences in the details of the ritual. Above all, the meaning and some of the secondary functions of the ceremony differ from tribe to tribe (see Bennett 1944).

The central theme of the Cheyenne Sun Dance is world renewal. As explained to G. A. Dorsey by a Cheyenne priest,

> The object of the ceremony is to make the whole world over again, and from the time the Lodge-maker makes his vow everything is supposed to begin to take on new life, for the Medicine-Spirit [Maiyun], having heard the prayer of the pledger, begins at once to answer it. When the man makes the vow, he does it not so much for himself or his family, as for the whole tribe. Attending upon his vow and its fulfillment is an abundance of good water and good breath of the wind, which is the same as the breath of the Medicine-Spirit who regards all things. At the time of the Lone-tipi, when the earth is first created, it is just beginning to grow. As the ceremony progresses, this earth increases in size, and when the lodge itself is erected we build a fire which represents the heat of the sun, and we place the lodge to face the east that the heavenly bodies may pass over it and fertilize it. (Dorsey 1905:II, 186)

The Cheyennes' own name for the Sun Dance embodies this notion in the word oxheheom, which means "New Life Lodge," or "Lodge of the Generator." Again, in the words of a Cheyenne priest,

> Formerly this dance represented only the creation of the earth. The Cheyenne grew careless and combined other things with the ceremony. At the time of the Lone-tipi, though everything is barren, the earth is beginning to grow. Now it has grown. Thus they make the earth, buffalo wallow,

grease, wool, and sinew to make growth. By the time of the end of the lodge things have grown, people have become happy; the world has reached its full growth, and people rejoice. When they use the bone whistle they are happy like the eagle, which is typical of all birds and of all happiness. (Dorsey 1905:II, 57)

The origin myth of the Sun Dance attributes its introduction among the Cheyennes to a second culture hero, Erect Horns (*Tomsivsi*). He, like Sweet Medicine, journeyed to a sacred mountain near a great body of water to receive instruction from Maiyun and the Thunder Spirit. Unlike Sweet Medicine, however, he undertook his pilgrimage because of the dire need of the people. The myth tells that long ago there was famine. "Vegetation withered, the animals starved, the land became barren and dry, and the ancient Cheyenne were on the verge of starvation, for they had no food but dried vegetation and their dogs of burden" (Dorsey 1905:I, 46). Erect Horns was a young man then known as Standing on the Ground and also as Rustling Corn. He selected the beautiful wife of the tribal chief to slip off secretly with him on a long journey which led to the Sacred Mountain. Inside the mountain the pair was taught the Sun Dance. At the end, the Great Spirit gave Erect Horns the sacred horned buffalo-skin hat whence comes his name.

The spirit's parting words were,

Follow my instructions accurately, and then, when you go forth from this mountain, all of the heavenly bodies will move. The Roaring Thunder will awaken them, the sun, moon, stars, and the rain will bring forth fruits of all kinds, all the animals will come forth behind you from this mountain, and they will follow you home. Take this horned cap to wear when you perform the ceremony that I have given you, and you will control the buffalo and all other animals. Put the cap on as you go from here and the earth will bless you. (Dorsey 1905:I, 48)

It was as it had been promised. When they came forth from the mountain, the entire earth turned fresh and new. The buffalo came forth to follow them to their homeland. The first Sun Dance was performed in accordance with Erect Horn's instructions, and all was well. The Buffalo Hat, which had been given to Erect Horns, is preserved to this day, and it constitutes the second great tribal fetish.

The Sun Dance was in fact introduced into Cheyenne culture by the Suhtai, who were another Algonkian-speaking tribe first contacted by the Cheyenne after they had crossed the Missouri River in their westward migration. The Suhtai and Cheyennes had at first fought each other, but later, on learning how similar were their tongues, they joined together and became one tribe. The Suhtai still retain distinctive customs in dress and other matters, and now form but one band among the ten of the Cheyenne. The Sun Dance prayers and songs are performed in the Suhtai dialect rather than in true Cheyenne. Thus, the separate culture heroes, sacred tribal fetishes, and their associated ceremonies have been integrated into the tribal culture as two homologous complexes.

The Sun Dance of the Cheyenne has been recorded in considerable detail by Dorsey (1905:II) and Grinnell (1923). For our purposes no more than a brief indication of its major aspects need be recounted.

The ceremony is pledged by an individual for the same personal reasons as lead a person to sponsor the Sacred Arrow Renewal. The dance is usually given in years when there is no Arrow Renewal, but if both are to be given in the same season, the Sun Dance follows the Arrow Renewal, which is the more important ceremony.

The Sun Dance requires eight days to complete. The first four days are given over to building the dance lodge and to secret rites in the Lone Tipi, which symbolizes the Sacred Mountain. The last four days are devoted to the public dance in the Sun Dance Lodge.

The pledger is called "The Reproducer" or "Multiplier," because through his act the tribe is reborn and increases in numbers. From the time of making the vow until the completion of the dance, the pledger and his wife must not express their sexual desires. Any intercourse on their part will cause them to die. In the origin myth, Erect Horns refused to have sexual relations with his beautiful companion until after they had emerged from the Sacred Mountain. In preparing the ceremony, the pledger is helped not so much by his relatives as by the members of his warrior society, who give many gifts to defray the expense, and who themselves participate in the dance. They also direct certain phases of the ceremony. First, they direct the positions of the different bands in the camp circle. More important, they select from among the former Sun Dance priests the one who will enact the role of the Great Spirit, who first taught the ceremony to Erect Horns. He is known as "The One Who Shows How," and he serves as the high priest of the rite. He is helped by an assistant high priest, who represents Thunder, the second teacher of Erect Horns. The other priests are those men who have previously pledged the rite and so have learned the mysteries of the Lone Tipi. All of these men together, including the pledger, are called "The Reanimators."

The four days in the Lone Tipi are replete with symbolic imagery and actions portraying earth renewal and continuance. Five separate "earths" are successively smoothed out on the ground. A buffalo skull is ritually consecrated through the insertion of balls of water grass in its eye sockets and nostrils. Many special pipe cleaners—sticks with a wad of buffalo hair—represent the life-sustaining buffalo and must be changed after the rituals at each "earth," because they would carry away some of the power of growth of the earth if moved from one to another. The wife of the pledger (or some other woman chosen by him, if for any reason, such as menstruation, his own wife may not serve) shares the rites in the Lone Tipi with the high priest, just as Erect Horns' female companion was in the Sacred Mountain with him. The Lone Tipi rites, like the Arrow Renewal Ceremony, end with a ritual, purificatory sweat bath for the priests.

The basic features of the public dance divide into four distinguishable parts: 1) the building of the lodge, 2) the priests' rituals, 3) dancing before the center pole, and 4) individual self-torture as a kind of sacrificial offering.

During the four preliminary days of the Lone Tipi rites, the remainder of the camp is not idle. The military society of the pledger, which is to dance as a body, sets up a tipi of one of its members in the open area within the circle. This and other societies rehearse Sun Dance songs; they feast and exchange presents. Various families exchange feasts and gifts. Purely social dances are held for the fun of it. There is much gaming, expressions of fun and happiness, and socializing. Such an atmosphere pervades the whole camp throughout the entire ceremony, except for the moments when the high priest and pledger's wife sexually consecrate themselves.

For the building of the lodge, a spy is first selected to find a suitable tree for the center pole. It must be some warrior who has penetrated into an enemy camp to scout them out on some occasion when the entire Cheyenne tribe was on the warpath. He selects the spot at which the center pole will be erected (somewhere out toward the front of the open area within the camp circle). Here he puts up a few willow boughs. Next he goes out on the "warpath" to find an "enemy." Stealthily penetrating a grove of trees, he spots a suitable tree, steals up on it and counts coup with his ax upon its trunk. (Coup is the French word meaning "blow." A coup is any honorable war deed at the expense of a Cheyenne enemy.) All this is done on the second and third days.

On the morning of the third day, the scout circles the camp before approaching the center pole markers. These he strikes and tells of the war exploit that qualified him for his select honor. Meanwhile, the braves of the different military societies are dressing and putting on their war paint. One after another, each society rides full tilt into the camp circle, whooping and shouting. Armed with willow spears and shields, they charge straight at the center pole boughs, striking them as they charge past, subsequently to engage in sham battles. Women, too, gather to count coup on the enemy. Then all go off to cut the timbers for the lodge. Each of four military societies brings in a specially painted pole to represent the four directions. It is a time of great excitement and high spirits.

The center pole is cut and transported ritually by chiefs only, for it represents the world and "the sunshine of all the world." It is the last of the upright poles to be put in place, and its raising is done with much ritual and sacrificial offerings. Bundles of dogwood and cottonwood brush are lashed between the two forks of what is to be the upper end of the center pole. They become the nest of the Thunder-bird, the spirit who controls the sun and rain, and is the chief of all birds. A broken arrow, symbolic of enemy arrows which are thus made useless, a bit of buffalo meat, symbolic of the major food supply, a rope representation of the morning star, and a phallic rawhide effigy of an enemy tribesman are added to the nest. In raising the pole, songs are sung which relate to the growth of the earth.

The completed lodge forms a large circle of upright posts around the center pole to which they are joined by stringers. The roof is partially covered over with valuable buffalo robes donated by qualified warriors. On the night of the day it is finished, the lodge is dedicated by the priests, who sing eight groups of ceremonial songs for the dancers who perform set and restrained rythmic patterns. Now the great act of regenerative consecration is offered. The chief priest and wife of the pledger step together over incense, enveloping themselves in a buffalo robe so that they will be thoroughly purified throughout their bodies by the sacred incense. This done, the priests all file from the lodge, led by the pledger's wife. To the east of the lodge and just inside the opening of the camp circle they stop. A solemn prayer is offered to Maiyun, to the spirits of the four directions, to the sun and stars. It asks their blessing on the entire world. It begs for the growth of the world, for animals, birds, and people, for blessing upon stones, trees, grass, and earth of all kinds, and that the sun shall shine and rain shall fall, as needed.

The priests return to the Sun Dance Lodge, leaving the high priest and pledger's wife alone. Now the Crier, who is one of the priests purified and painted, calls upon all the world to listen as he announces the right of the high priest to perform the ritual act he is about to do on behalf of the tribe. The priest and pledger's wife draw the buffalo robe about themselves, incensing their bodies again. They sing the sacred pipe song and "grow" the earth, raising the sacred pipe skyward four times. Within the robe they then have sex relations, so that all that lives may be born. Now the dance proper may begin.

In the dancing, the participants face the center pole, rising up and down on their toes while standing in one place. As they rise, they blow piping, short blasts upon eagle-wing bone whistles held between their teeth. Those who can endure it to the end do so almost continuously (with but brief periods of rest and without food or water) for four nights and days. On each day, they are ceremonially painted with a series of symbolic painted patterns applied by ceremonial grandfathers.

On the following day, the priests, assisted by the wives of the pledger and high priest, go through an elaborate ritual of building an altar within the dance lodge. It is built around the sacred buffalo skull that had been prepared in the Lone Tipi, and includes five pieces of sod (growing grass) symbolic of the five great directional spirits, arched sticks (rainbows), brush (the matured vegetation for which they have prayed in the Lone Tipi), and a sand-painting symbol of the morning star in red, black, yellow, and white sand. Peeled sticks, painted white and representing scalped enemies, are there, too, as are feathered, red and black painted sticks representing the Cheyennes.

The altar symbolizes the fifth earth made in the priests' rituals; it is the completed and realized earth toward which the whole ceremony is directed— an earth replete with green life and buffalo, sunshine and rainbows, beneficent spirits, healthy Cheyennes and defeated enemies. It is the supreme hope.

To the untutored outsider who sees the public aspects of the Cheyenne Sun Dance, the most spectacular part (and in the view of a number of early reporters, a horrifying thing) is the voluntary self-torture undertaken by a number of the men. Self-torture is practiced by a number of northern Plains tribes as a form of religious sacrifice, but none carry it to the degree practiced by the Cheyennes. A few of the dancers in the Sun Dance Lodge may indulge in it, but most of the sufferers perform their acts of self-sacrifice outside of the lodge. The sacrifice is done as the result of a voluntarily made individual vow as a means to obtain the "pity" of supernatural spirits in the hope of obtaining good fortune. The act also brings great public approval and is a conspicuous means of gaining social prestige.

The self-sacrifice in the dance lodge is known as "hanging from the center pole." One who has vowed to do this asks a medicine man who has himself made the same sacrifice to help him. The medicine man fastens the end of two ropes to the crotch of the center pole, adjusting them so that they will reach just to the breast height of a standing man. He next punches or cuts two holes in the skin just above each nipple. A small skewer is pushed through each pair of holes so that a narrow strip of skin laps over it and holds it against the breast. The free ends of the rope are fastened about the skewers. The sacrificer may then dance, fastened to the pole, all through the night, and if by morning he has not succeeded in tearing the skin loose so as to free himself, his medicine man cuts the skin off, and his ordeal is ended. Or, if the sacrificer wishes to achieve his end in one sudden burst, he may suddenly strain back on the ropes in an effort to tear the skewers free at once. There are variations and elaborations on this pattern: skewers may be put through the flesh of the face over the cheekbones just below the eyes; skewers from which are hung buffalo skulls may be put into the shoulders and over the shoulder blades on the back. Those who do not wish to sacrifice themselves in the lodge will have skewers put in their backs. Ropes are hung from the skewers, and as many as from one to fifteen buffalo skulls are attached to the ropes. The sacrificer drags these along the ground around the camp circle. If the catching of the horns of the skulls in brush and grass does not cause the thongs to tear loose, the flesh is cut to release them when the sacrificer has trudged as long or as far as he has vowed.

Such self-sacrifice does not contribute to the earth-renewal purposes of the Sun Dance, nor is it done on behalf of the tribe as a whole. It may be vowed to help cure a relative or to avert danger in war. Or it may be undertaken as the result of a dream. The psychological basis of these practices will be discussed in Chapter 9.

The Massaum (Contrary) or Animal Dance

The third of the great tribal ceremonies is very different in quality from the Arrow Renewal and Sun Dance, although it, too, is intended to insure well-being—that is, plenty of meat. It is mainly a hunting ritual taught to Sweet Medicine when·he visited the Sacred Mountain. He, in turn, brought it to the Cheyennes. Women play a much more important role throughout the Massaum.

Four days and nights are given over to closed rites in a double-sized skin tipi raised about a center pole on which green boughs have been left, "that all the trees and grass and fruits may grow strong." The pledger and his wife are under the instruction of a priest who has previously pledged the dance.

There are the many ritual movements of smoking, painting, and so forth (described in detail in Grinnell 1923:II, 285-334). In this case, all activity centers on preparing and painting a wolf skin to be worn by the pledger on the fifth and final day.

In private lodges, various men who have dreamed of some animal acting in a peculiar way get a group of their friends ritually to dress up in imitation of this animal. On the fourth day, women build a symbolic antelope or buffalo corral—a shaded pen of upright poles with two diverging arms of brush extending out toward the opening of the camp circle.

Two wolves are the main ritual animals, but on the fifth day other groups join in—buffalo, elk, deer, foxes, mountain lions, horses, bears, antelope, coyotes, and cranes and blackbirds. The men of each group run, dance, and act like the animal they represent. The animals run about, "hunted" by members of the Bowstring Society, or Contrary Warriors, who do things backwards and are the bravest of the brave. In the Animal Dance, they clown and cut up to the delight of the people watching. Hence, the dance is called Massaum, derived from *massa'ne,* crazy. At various points, the animals enter the corral, which is just what the Cheyenne want the animals to do when they use this method of hunting (see pp. 65-66). All this mimicry and clowning, which occurs on the final day, involves a great amount of high jinks and sporting fun, and is thus a great contrast to the heavy solemnity of the Arrow Renewal and the strenuous self-sacrifice of the Sun Dance. The four days and nights of preliminary rites, however, are not unlike those preceding the Sun Dance in general character and in details (including, *apparently,* the sexual dedication of the pledger's wife with the instructing high priest).

Whichever dance, or dances, may be given in any particular year, when the ceremony is over the whole tribe is ready to move off on the great summer buffalo hunt. Their spirits are high and they are ready to act as one body, confident now in their powers, for the whole earth and all upon it has been reinvigorated in their favor, and their mastery over their environment and all the animals in it is complete.

PART TWO

Social Structure

2

Family, Kindred, and Band

✓

B Y SOCIAL STRUCTURE is meant the ways in which groups and individuals are organized and relate to each other in the functioning entity that is the society. Among the Cheyennes the most significant groups are the family, kindred, band, military fraternities, women's societies, and the tribal council of forty-four peace chiefs.

Courtship and Marriage

Marriage, for the Cheyennes, is a formal and serious matter. The Cheyennes are sexually repressed, have very strict notions of proper conduct, and are most sensitive to what other members of the tribe think of them. In the story of her life, a Cheyenne woman told Truman Michelson:

> My mother would always tell me that the main purpose of her teaching me, as well as the object of my owning my own bed, was to keep me at home, and to keep me from being away to spend my nights with my girl chum. This was done so that there would be no chance for gossip by other people. (Michelson 1932:2)

When, as a girl, this woman first began to get the attentions of a beau, her father's sister came to her lodge to instruct her in how a girl should act and to stress the importance of proper behavior. Even when marriage was finally achieved, the situation did not change very much. "After I was married I thought I would have more freedom in going around with my girl friends, but my mother watched me more closely and kept me near my husband, day and night. This was done to prevent any gossip from my husband's people" (Michelson 1932:7).

Her statement was not idle talk, nor was hers an unusual instance, for Grinnell is not overstating the case when he writes,

The women of the Cheyennes are famous among all western tribes for their chastity. In old times it was most unusual for a girl to be seduced, and she who had yielded was disgraced forever. The matter at once became known, and she was taunted with it wherever she went. It was never forgotten. No young man would marry her. (Grinnell 1923:I, 156)

Under such circumstances Cheyenne courting is a bashful and long, drawn-out affair. It usually takes four or five years for a young man to win his bride, and when he is ready to put the question it is directed to her family and not to the girl. What is more, good form requires that the young man not do the asking himself but rather send an old female or other relatives in his stead. After adolescence, boys and girls do not associate with each other, so there is no direct opportunity to develop camaraderie. Once a boy has seen a girl whom he hopes to make his sweetheart, he approaches her furtively. He knows the path from her family lodge to the stream where she gets water or the grove where she gathers wood. Hopefully, he stands along the path. As she passes, he gives her robe a little tug. Perhaps he feels this is too bold. If so, he whistles or calls to her. She may stonily ignore him, much to his mortification. Or she may make the stars shine by stopping to talk about this and that, but never of love. If all goes well, they may later begin to meet and talk outside her lodge. In time, they may exchange rings (either the old-time horn ones or those of metal obtained from traders) that young people wear. They are then engaged. Except for the exchange of rings, a suitor rarely gives presents directly to a girl. When the time comes, these go to her male relatives.

Tootling on a medicine flute is supposed to be a means of casting a love spell over a reluctant maiden. Certain medicine men can concoct a spruce gum to help a hapless swain to win his goal. If the girl chews the gum, her thoughts cannot leave the boy who gives it to her.

In the course of time, a suitor makes his intention known to his close kindred. If they do not agree that the match is a good one, they will refuse to assist him. If they approve, they bring together such items as clothing, blankets, guns, bows and arrows, and horses. One or more elderly respected men or women are selected to lead the horses piled with gifts over to the tipi of the girl's parents. The horses are staked outside. The emissary enters, smokes, talks small talk, finally puts the question, and then goes home without waiting for the answer. This is because the girl's family has to have time to talk the matter over. Her father or brother, as the case may be, sends for her male kindred, who convene at her tipi to discuss the pros and cons of the match. Should they decide against it, the horses are led back to the suitor. Should they decide "Yes," the goods are unloaded and distributed among the relatives. On the next day, they all convene again, bringing gifts equivalent in worth to what each has received. While the women of the family paint and outfit the girl in her finest buckskin dress, the men load their gifts on the horses that are to be returned in exchange for those already received. The finest horse of all is reserved as the bride's mount. Thus richly caparisoned, she is led to the lodge of her husband-to-be by an old woman not a relative. Her mother follows, leading the gift horses. At the groom's lodge, his young relatives and friends place the bride on a blanket, carry her through the door, and bestow her in the place of honor at the rear of the tipi. There her new female in-laws re-dress her in the new clothes they have made for the occasion, redo her hair, and repaint her. A feast follows.

In the days following, both mothers work at providing a new household. It is the girl's mother's privilege to provide a new tipi and its furnishing. Relatives from both sides help with many contributions. When all is ready, the lodge is set up, usually in the vicinity of the bride's mother's lodge (uxorilocal residence). The couple then leave the husband's tipi for their own. Thus is a new secondary conjugal family founded (the primary conjugal family being the one into which a person is born).

The Kindred

The next largest social unit in Cheyenne society is that of the kindred. This is the group that customarily camps together within the band encampment. As a settlement, it consists of the lodge (or lodges, if the family head has several wives) of the family head, plus the lodges of his daughters and their husbands, and other relatives. The sons-in-law are expected to be the main providers of meat for all the group, which is cooked in the mother's lodge and carried by the daughters to their own tipis for eating. Although they live so near, the sons-in-law are expected nonetheless to avoid seeing their mother-in-law, and under no circumstances should they speak directly to her.

In spite of the importance of women, Cheyenne uxorilocal residence has not resulted in the formation of matrilineages or matrilineal clans. Grinnell, it is true, thought he detected evidence of an old-time matrilineal organization among the Cheyennes, but the evidence is hardly convincing. The brief stay of the Cheyennes among the matrilineal village tribes of the upper Missouri River Valley may have planted the beginnings of matrilineality in Cheyenne culture, but the episode of earth-lodge village life with sedentary horticulture was too brief to allow the pattern to develop.

The kinship structure of the Cheyennes is strictly bilateral; its emphasis is on horizontal classification along generation levels rather than vertically along lineage lines (Eggan 1955:71). The Cheyennes draw no distinction between siblings and cousins. Within the primary conjugal family an emphasis on seniority is reflected in a distinction between elder brother (*na'niha*) and younger (*na:sima*), and elder sister (*namhan*) and younger (*na:sima*). The younger brothers and sisters are not distinguished from each other in terminology. Relative age is more important than the sex of the person referred to (if that person is younger). Hence, *na:sima* means younger sibling of either sex. The age distinction does not apply in the case of cousins, however; all of them are called either "brother" or "sister."

A Cheyenne calls his father, father's brother, and all known male cousins of his father *nihu'*. But the mother's brother, who perforce belongs to a different kindred, is called *naxan*. Although for convenience we have translated *nihu'* as father, what it really means to a Cheyenne is "male member of my male progenitor's kindred and generation." Father and paternal uncles are considered together as kinsmen of the same order, while maternal uncles are terminologically identified as being in a different category.

Mother, mother's sister, and mother's female cousins are all called *na'go'*, while father's sisters and father's female cousins are distinguished as *nahan*.

On the generation level of grandparents a Cheyenne draws no distinction other than sex: grandfather and grandmother, just as in the Anglo-American kinship system. Two generations below him, a Cheyenne makes no distinctions whatsoever. All related children are called *nixa*, grandchild.

A Cheyenne calls his own children *na:'* (son) and *na'ts* (daughter). He also calls the children of his brothers and male cousins by the same terms. In other words, they are equated with his own offspring. All are child members of the same extended family. The children of his sisters and female cousins he calls "nephew" and "niece." They are set apart. When a Cheyenne woman is talking, she calls her sisters' and female cousins' children by the son and daughter terms, while *she* sets apart the children of her brothers and male cousins as nephew and niece. Consequently, when a male is speaking, *na:'* and *na'ts* mean more than "son" and "daughter"; they mean "offspring of my male relatives of my own generation." What we have for convenience called "nephew" and "niece" really mean "offspring of my female relatives of my own generation." They must be called by a different term from that used by a Cheyenne to identify his own children; if they were called the same as son and daughter, it would logically imply that a man was producing children by his sisters—and that is forbidden by the incest prohibitions.

If the reader has grasped the nature of the way a Cheyenne groups his relatives as revealed by relationship terms, he will see that five things stand out as distinctive in the kinship structure: 1) both parents' kindred are equally important to the individual. He does not socially or legally belong to one group and not the other. There is no unilineal descent group. All kin of his own generation, whether descended on the mother's side or the father's are "brother" and "sister." 2) On the parental level, mother's brother and father's sister are given special terms, since they cannot marry one's "mother" or "father" and because they belong to different kindred from the father and mother respectively. 3) "Sons" and "daughters" and "nephews" and "nieces" belong to the same kindred, but have to be distinguished because of the implications of the incest taboo. 4) All "grandchildren" are lumped together, since, from the speaker's point of view, they are all members of the same extended kindred. 5) Grandparents are also lumped for the same reason as grandchildren.

The Cheyennes, therefore, tend to draw as few distinctions as possible between relatives, except for distinctions between generations (although Petter estimates that the twenty-eight relationship terms *can* be modified in over 20,000 ways [Petter 1915:900]). This is consonant with the emphasis on seniority in social relations which is so important in the authority system of their culture. As was shown in the first chapter, they think of the tribe as one large family (the camp circle, for example, symbolizes the family tipi). They extend the concept of the family as widely as possible. Marriage is much more a family than an individual matter. Family relations tend to be collective rather than individual.

Within the kinship group, however, the different statuses call for special modes of customary behavior. Husbands and wives, although they are diffident in their attitudes toward each other in the early stages of their marriages, usually become most fond of each other. They form a close working team with a strong sense of family responsibility. Michelson's old woman informant related, "We had our first child after we had been married a year. It was at that time that I began really to love my husband. He always treated me with respect and kindness" (Michelson 1932: 8). And when her husband died, "His death made me very lonely, and it was the most terrible event in my life." Such was the ideal life between husbands and wives, although, of course, it did not always work out thus. Some wives were shrewish. Some men were jealous or mean tempered. A story is told of one such man, Brave Wolf.

Brave Wolf was jealous of his wife's good looks. He would hear people remarking, "There is a woman who has two children and still holds her looks." These were children she had had by her former husband, High-backed Wolf, who had been killed by the Crows. Angered one day, Brave Wolf whipped his wife, Corn Woman, and when the camp moved, he left her behind. Brave Wolf's nephew, Sun's Road, then a single man, came by and heard her weeping. He went to his lodge to get his horse to bring the woman along. He brought her into the main camp that evening. Brave Wolf heard that she was there and came over to take up where he had left off. He began whipping her in her face.

Digging Bear, his niece, watched for her chance. She struck his arm with a club and numbed it as he raised it to swing his whip. He cried out, "Wait until my arm stops hurting! I'll fix you." Digging Bear told Corn Woman to get into the lodge. Brave Wolf got over his hurt and followed her into the lodge to whip her some more.

His niece started cracking his shins with a club.

"It's funny," Brave Wolf said, "that you children are taking the part of a woman not any relation to you. I am your uncle."

"Well, if you hadn't thumped our mother, we would not have done so." (Brave Wolf was their father's cousin and was hence called "father"; his wife was therefore their classificatory "mother," even though not a genetic relative.) Brave Wolf then took Corn Woman home, but the next morning he was thumping her again, so she ran away to hide in a gulch, covering herself with grass. Brave Wolf went riding up and down looking for her, with no success. When she thought she was safe, she went out and hid in a patch of boulders. The camp moved on in time, and she was left alone there starving.

After some time, a big wolf came up and asked her what was the trouble (he could speak good Cheyenne).

"My husband has been beating me, and I ran away."

"Well," the wolf told her, "I'll get you back safely."

He brought her meat, and warned her when a bear came by, so that she got safely up in a tree and could stay there until the bear went away. An elk came and talked to her, too. He gave her elk power.

Meantime, Brave Wolf went into mourning for her. Everyone in the camp thought she had committed suicide. Brave Wolf also joined the Contraries (a small group of recklessly brave men, who, as mentioned earlier, do everything backwards). He got a Contrary lance made by High Forehead. Only single men may have such a lance, but when Corn Woman left Brave Wolf, he was single again. He tried to get himself killed in battle, but Contrary lances are very lucky and this one carried him safely through battles. He could not get himself killed.

After a long time, the wolf led Corn Woman back to the Cheyenne camp. The wolf and the woman sat on a high hill overlooking the camp. "Over there is the camp," said the wolf. "A man will come out to look for you. You can't see him. Now I leave you. From now on, always put out some meat for me each morning." For the rest of her days, Corn Woman made the offering to the wolf who had saved her; he was her guardian spirit. When the wolf left her, she "came to." Later, she told people she thought she had almost turned into a wolf herself.

Now she started down the hill through a gulch, and she met a young man. He saw her in her disheveled condition. No clothes but a small piece of blanket for covering. No hair comb. Her hair in a mess. She was weak and emaciated from lack of proper food. The sight of him made her weaker. She staggered. The young man was so sorry for her that he wept in pity. She tried to, too. But no tears or voice would come.

"You stay right here," he said. "Your brother is hunting right over there. I'll bring him."

He found Crazy Head, her brother, and told him, "Your sister is right over here."

Crazy Head and the hunters rushed over and found her. They carried her back to the camp on a horse, so weak she could hardly stay on it.

Brave Wolf heard the news. He came in, his hair cut in mourning style. He ran up and started to hug his former wife. She bit his arm.

That made Crazy Head mad. He wanted to kill Brave Wolf, because he had made his sister remain away for so long. Then Corn Woman's mother came up and started to beat Brave Wolf. All the people began beating him. When they got back in camp, all the women beat him.

Brave Wolf was infatuated with Corn Woman. He wanted her back. He kept sending horses for her, but Crazy Head's people would throw sticks at them and drive them away. Corn Woman's mother would insult the women who brought them. When Brave Wolf came around, Corn Woman's sister would strike him on the forehead and taunt him, saying, "You look more like a mountain sheep than a man." He made no effort to protect himself, but would only drop his head and take the blows.

Brave Wolf was a great fighter, not then a chief, though he was later. He had a fine black war pony that everyone wanted, but he would not trade it or give it away.

On the warpath, he took to cooking for Sun's Road, Corn Woman's brother. He did everything for him, just as though he were a servant.

One time, when Crazy Head was leading a war party, Brave Wolf brought Sun's Road a nice roast. He was leading the famous bob-tailed black. "You know I have ridden this horse in war. You know this horse's qualities as well as I do," he told Sun's Road. "Now I want you to have him to ride in war. What is more, I want you to have my Contrary lance, if you will take it." These were his greatest possessions.

When they were back from the war party, Sun's Road spoke to his mother, "You know that when a man is leading a war party he is apt to go pretty hungry so that his men will have enough to eat. Brave Wolf has done all these pitiful things for me. I have known all the time what he wants. He wants my sister back. You had better put up an extra lodge. My sister will go back to him. You tell her to get ready."

When her mother told her what Sun's Road had said, Corn Woman wept. "I never thought I would marry that man again, but if my brother says I must go, I must. My brother is a great fighter. If I say, 'No,' he'll probably get himself killed in the first fight (a protest suicide). Then I'll think how I caused it."

When they were together again, she told Brave Wolf, "Don't you ever try to beat me again. If you do, I'll fight you with whatever is at hand. I don't care if you kill me."

From that time on, he was her slave.

This case history, which was told by Calf Woman (who was in the camp at the time) and confirmed by High Forehead, illustrates a number of aspects of Cheyenne society. First, Cheyennes, like any other human beings, are not automatic slaves of custom; there are always those who deviate from the norms of right conduct. But the Cheyennes as a group have an unusually strong sense of proper form and they are not prone to let misconduct pass lightly. Second, the wrong-doing Cheyenne who repents, is contrite, and is willing to make amends, is rehabilitated with the cooperation of his fellows and restored to his former state. Third, Cheyenne women, although their status is inferior to men in many respects, are strong willed and aggressive; they are by no means downtrodden. Fourth, the Cheyenne male who finds the stress of life too much may find an institutionalized way open to glory and public esteem by becoming a Contrary, or more simply by getting himself killed in battle, dying the glorious death. Fifth, brothers have an absolute right of disposition of their sisters in marriage, a right that takes precedence even over the father's (Corn Woman said she was afraid she would be responsible for her brother's suicide by death in battle if she did not accede to his decision).

The brother-sister relationship is one of formal respect and restraint. Although they may play together as small children, beginning at puberty they must shed all manifestations of familiarity. There can be no physical contacts or joking between them. No obscenities may be uttered in each other's presence. Indeed, they may not even speak to each other. There is an indirect way around this tabu, however. A man who goes to his brother-in-law's tipi to borrow something, for instance, may find that the brother-in-law is not at home. He does not tell his sister what he wants, but he can tell her little baby of his request. After a while his sister, having overheard his wish, puts the article in a place where it can be seen. He picks it up and departs. He has obtained what he wants without violating the amenities of right conduct.

The incest tabu applies rigorously to brothers and sisters, and governs all their conduct. This is consonant both with Cheyenne distrust of sex and with the universal functional bases of the incest tabus. It also correlates with the power of disposal in marriage that a brother may exercise over his sister. So great is this authority, and so serious an affront to a young brave's ego is its flaunting, that if a sister disobeys his word, a brother may actually commit suicide (and there have been such cases). In such a case, the girl is disowned by her family. Pemmican Road's sister was driven from the tribe for disobeying her brother. Many years later, she returned to the Northern Cheyenne. When people came to tell her father, the famous chief, Iron Shirt, that his daughter had returned, he stonily replied, "I do not know how many years have passed since I disowned her for disobeying her brother. She is not my daughter. I do not want to see her." She tried again later, but he never took her in. "Pemmican Road died without father or mother" (Llewellyn and Hoebel 1941:174-175).

A woman divorces her husband simply by moving back into her parents' tipi. A man may divorce his wife by drumming her away at the so-called Omaha Dance. At one point in the dance, those men who have drummed a wife away dance as a group. A man who wants publicly to shame his wife may join them. At the end of the dance he strikes the drum, crying, "I throw her away." When a man is made a leader of the Omaha Dance, the greatest gesture he can make is to throw his sister away. "It was like giving away a fine horse, only more so." In contrast to a wife so divorced, the sister is supposed to be highly honored. When a brother strikes the drum, he throws the stick among the men, and the man whom it hits becomes the sister's husband.

Mothers continually admonish, exhort, and train their daughters. Fathers are friendly with their sons, but do little about their education until they are of age; boys are pretty much on their own and learn from each other until it is time to go on the warpath. It is a father's sister who has the freer relation to a child. She makes the infant's cradle and gives it gifts throughout life. She lightly teases the children in a way a mother never does. A niece may make jokes in return and may use any of the aunt's property without asking, if she needs it. Throughout life, a niece gives her aunt presents in exchange for her privileges. All in all, the relation of children, both male and female, to their father's sister is free of the formal restraints they are made to feel toward their mother. "I would prefer to have an aunt around any time rather than my mother," was the way High Forehead summed it up. Mother's sisters are "mothers" and treated accordingly.

A maternal uncle has much the same relation to his nieces and nephews as does the father's sister. Unlike the system in many American Indian tribes in which he, rather than the father, punishes an unruly boy (Pettitt 1946: 18-24), a Cheyenne mother's brother, although he will talk to the boy, will never punish him. Mothers sometimes lose patience with their daughters and strike them. In two recorded cases in which this happened, the daughter hanged herself and the mother was banished for murder; after these events the Arrows were renewed (Llewellyn and Hoebel 1941:161-162).

Cheyenne grandparents are the great indulgers of the children. Allowing for the differences in their ages, grandparents and grandchildren are real comrades and treat each other quite as equals. Grandfathers pass the tribal lore and myths to their descendants.

In-law relations are of a different order. Cheyennes like to accrue relatives and they welcome the enlargement of their kinship bonds through marriage. It is because this is so important to them that the families take such care in approving and selecting the mates for their youngsters. In any society there is always an undercurrent of psychological hostility between in-laws. In some, such as Dobu, the hostility is overt and institutionally manifest (Fortune 1932). In Cheyenne culture, however, the institutions of social structure are devised to minimize and control the hostility while at the same time building up the cooperative aspects of the relationship.

A Cheyenne male calls his sister's husband *nitov*. He also calls his wife's brother by the same term. The term, which is equivalent to our "brother-in-law" descriptively means "brother through marriage or affinity." Brothers-in-law are expected to be rough and ready pals. They give assistance to each other (as the suitor on the warpath), exchange presents from time to time, and work together. This is the cooperative side. Hostility, on the other hand, is vicariously released through rough joking and horseplay. Once when the camp crier was making the rounds calling the tribal chiefs to council, Bull Head cried out, "Don't call them chiefs! Call them fools. There are too many fools with the chiefs." This was not blasphemy, for his brother-in-law was a chief; when I was told this anecdote by Last Walker, the other Cheyennes in the tent roared with laughter. It was a good brother-in-law joke, an expression of privileged familiarity much appreciated.

A man's attitude toward his sisters-in-law is much like that toward brothers-in-law. They joke and are more than free and easy in their. overt relations. The relations are just the opposite to those that exist between brother and sister. The incest tabu that restrains siblings is not present in this relationship; every sister-in-law is a potential second wife to a Cheyenne man, since the tribe practices preferential levirate and sororate marriage. Because the ties between the two families have already been cemented by marriage, the circumspect behavior of a boy courting his first wife-to-be need not apply in sister-in-law relations.

Behavior toward a man's mother-in-law, however, is quite a different matter. She is absolutely tabued to him. Although he has to furnish her household with meat and perform other services, he may never, never speak to her. He should never be alone with her, and when he is in her presence, he should cover his head. Familiarity is out of the question and the opportunities for development of friction between them are reduced to a minimum.

For some Cheyennes, however, the situation can be otherwise. A man who has performed well in all things receives considerable social approbation when he selects one of the horses he has taken in war to give to his mother-in-law. The presentation, of course, is made through another person. His mother-in-law may then return the honor, if she is a member of the Women's Quilling Society. To do this she makes him a fine buffalo robe embroidered in dyed porcupine quills, which she formally presents to him at a feast for the Quilling Society held in her own lodge. He does not partake of the feast but leaves with the robe on a horse which has been staked outside the lodge by his mother-in-law as a gift for him. From this time on, the mother-in-law–son-in-law tabu is set aside for them.

This road is not open to many Cheyennes. It is a class privilege and a high achievement that may be grasped only by those who have shown the best character—the young man who has shown himself worthy in all areas, the woman of good family whose personal excellence is shown by her membership in the Quillers. Apparently, the fear of misbehavior and trouble that the existence of the tabu implies is adequately dissipated in a feeling of assurance that these two will not misbehave. The possibility of setting it aside shows also that the Cheyennes look upon the mother-in-law tabu as something onerous but necessary for the ordinary man.

A Cheyenne father-in-law may speak to his son-in-law, but he should not try to boss him. The young man's attitude is one of reserved respect.

Tylor long ago demonstrated that the forms of parent-in-law avoidance are correlated to the patterns of residence. Avoidance of the mother-in-law by a man is more common where uxorilocal residence (near the bride's parents) is the custom. A woman avoids her father-in-law more commonly where virilocal residence (near the groom's parents) is the mode. Since the Cheyenne normally are uxorilocal, we would expect the avoidance rules to be less stringent, if not entirely absent, in the case of a woman and her father-in-law. Such is, indeed, the case. A daughter-in-law must show respect and reserve in her associations with her husband's father, but both are allowed to speak to each other and to be in the same lodge together.

Because there is no need for inhibition of sexual impulses between a woman and her husband's mother, they may associate together freely, although the younger woman should behave with deference, "in the best way," as one Cheyenne put it to Eggan (Eggan 1955:55).

Parent-in-law and child-in-law relations are psychologically softened through the attitudes associated with kinship terminology. Son-in-law and daughter-in-law are both referred to by the grandchild term, *nixa*. Thus, they are brought within the speaker's kindred and closely linked by more than in-law bonds. The behavior between them is not, however, that of grandparent-grandchild. The younger people refer to their parents-in-law by special terms of relationship which are derived from the words for grandparents but are nonetheless different. They express an impulse to fuse the older in-laws in the speaker's kindred while yet giving cultural recognition to the fact that they do after all belong to different kindred.

In sum, the Cheyennes do much to emphasize identity with families to which they are linked through marriage. They formally differentiate customary attitudes and behavior toward the different categories of affinal relatives in accordance with the functional requirements and variations allowed with respect to incest prohibitions and sexual repression, the maintenance of authority in the older generations, preferential marriage possibilities, and residence.

The Cheyenne kindred weaves its individual families into a finely knit cooperative body within which personal relations are carefully defined and formally controlled. For the Cheyennes, the kindred is more important than the inner circle of parents and children (Petter 1915:464). Age brings respect and authority but all relations are on a basis of mutual regard and assistance. The details of economic cooperation and division of labor will be presented in a later chapter.

Families and kindred differ in social prestige. As Grinnell writes, "Family rank . . . depended on the estimation in which the family was held by the best people. A good family was one that produced brave men and good sensible women, and that possessed more or less property. A brave and successful man has raised his family from low to very high rank; or a generation of inefficient men might cause a family to retrograde" (Grinnell 1923:I, 129). The Cheyennes with whom I worked gave the following characteristics of a good family: 1) it has plenty of good riding horses (forty or fifty of them); 2) the wife is a good housekeeper who keeps everything about the tipi neat and clean, is always good natured, and gets up every morning in the same mood; 3) it has plenty of parfleches stocked with dried meat, possible (ditty) bags, and long fringed saddle bags, good clothes and robes, all "up to date" and in good order; 4) it raises nice children, "those who act right, speak respectfully to elders, etc." A poor family is thought to be one in which the man is a poor rustler (that is, has no ability to take enemy horses), has only three or four horses, probably saddle worn and footsore from overuse. It has only a little food, a small tipi, and only enough clothes and robes to keep them warm. "Some poor men were hard workers but had no luck. People sometimes blame the wife. He rustles well, but she is wasteful" (Hoebel, n.d.).

Kindreds that are accustomed to camp on occasion by themselves apart from the main band of which they are members tend to form what might be recognized as embryo bands. Because these groups often have their own names, some early writers confused them with bands. Such groups are the Bear People, *nakoimana,* the White Cunning, *wokpotsit*—a reputedly quarrelsome group, hard to get along with—and the Northward Facing, *notamin.* The Shy People, *tatoimana,* originated when their family headman, Buffalo Chief, was exiled for killing two fellow tribesmen on different occasions. A number of his kindred followed him into exile and became markedly bashful and diffident when they met up with other Cheyennes. Although this event occurred some hundred and fifty years ago, these people still live as an identifiable group in one corner of the Tongue River Indian Reservation in Montana. Contemporary Cheyenne say they still tend to keep to themselves.

The Band

As the individual family is a unit of organization within its kindred, the kindred is a unit of organization within the band, or camp. Traditionally, each band has its designated location in the camp circle but there is no perfect agreement among present-day Cheyennes as to band location in the past. Cheyenne social organization goes through a semiannual cycle, for it is impossible with their type of economy for the Cheyennes to feed their total population during the fall, winter, and spring unless they disperse the tribe. In the summer, following the integration rites of the great tribal rituals, the tribe is together as a body during the period of the communal hunt, or on the infrequent occasions when it moves en masse against an enemy tribe (see pp. 72-73). From October to June it is broken up into band camps that scatter to parts of the Cheyenne territory where adequate winter forage for the horses is available and hunters may cover a wider range in search of game.

The core of a band consists of one or several closely related kindreds, although some families not directly related may choose to live with some particular band. The one great exception is the Dog Soldier band, the most powerful of the Cheyenne military societies. This group began living together as a unit at some time in the past and formed a band not at all based on kinship ties. The leaders of the bands are the outstanding heads of the several kindred who make up the band. They may or may not be tribal chieftains or chiefs of one of the military societies. The head chief of a large band is almost certain to be a tribal chief, a member of the Council of Forty-four (see Chapter 4).

There are ten main Cheyenne bands, as follows:

1. Eaters, *omisis*. The Eaters say they got their name because their ancestors were such great hunters that they always had plenty of food. Other Cheyenne say it is because they will eat anything. The Eaters are the largest Cheyenne band and live in the north.

2. Burnt Aorta, *heviqsnipahis*. This name is believed to have originated in a past emergency situation in which a roasted aorta from the heart of a buffalo was used as a tobacco pipe. The women of this band have the habit of sitting with their feet to the left. All other Cheyenne women sit with their feet on the right.

3. Hair Rope Men, *hevatanui*. While other Cheyenne use rawhide ropes, this band customarily makes its ropes of twisted hair.

4. Scabby, *oivimana*. Originally a kindred within the Hair Rope band, their headman, according to one account, developed a skin infection from using a mangy buffalo hide as a saddle blanket. Others in the family got the affliction from him. This happened around 1840.

5. Ridge Men, *isiometanui*. Another offshoot of the Hair Rope Men, who developed a preference for living in the "ridge country" at the head of the Smoky River in Colorado.

6. Prognathous Jaws, *oktouna*. Distinguished by its practice of a dance, preliminary to going on the warpath, known as the Deer Dance.

7. Poor, *haunowa*. Origin of the name unknown.

8. Dog Men, *hotamitanui*. Actually a military society, it became simultaneously a band when all the men of the Grey Hair, or Wrinkled Up, *masikota*, band joined the Dog society en masse. There is said to be a large proportion of gray-haired children in this group.

9. Suhtai. The band derived from the Suhtai tribe that joined up with the Cheyenne late in the eighteenth century.

10. Sioux-eaters (Those Who Eat With the Sioux), *wutapiu*. The name of this band is the Siouxan word for Eaters. It originates from the incorporation of a Sioux group into the Cheyenne tribe at some time in the past.

It is interesting to note in the names of the Cheyenne bands a total absence of any totemic identification with plants or animals. The names are nicknames, pure and simple. They do, however, reveal the important point that a society's culture is not a homogeneous leaven; subgroups have their subcultures. Bands retain their distinctive identity within the whole by persistently maintaining their own unique customs in some areas of daily living.

It is also worth noting that almost all the Cheyenne emphasis in the building of mythological accounts of the origins of their institutions is focused on the tribal structure and not on the bands. The elaborate culture-hero cycles of the adventures and innovations of Sweet Medicine and Erect Horns explain and justify the Medicine Arrow complex, Sun Dance, and Military Societies. Another myth accounts in detail for the formation of the tribal council. On the other hand, what Malinowski calls "the charters of institutions" are unformulated in the case of Cheyenne bands. The legends that ascribe the origins of band names are trivial and trite, often ambiguous and uncertain.

3

The Military Societies

CUTTING ACROSS the kindreds and bands are the sodalities, or clubs, of the warriors (the Dog Soldiers are the exception). While hunting is a male activity woven into the interests of the family, fighting was an activity institutionalized in the organization of the military societies. The interests of these societies were tribal rather than kin based.

The societies are not organized trainbands of the order of colonial militia in the early days of American settlement. They are, in their way, somewhat more comparable to local American Legion or V.F.W. posts—social and civic organizations mainly centered on the common experience of the members as warriors, with rituals glorifying and enhancing that experience, and with duties and services performed on behalf of the community at large.

The idea of the military societies is attributed to a mythological female founder of the Cheyenne governmental structure (see Chapter 4); Sweet Medicine is said to have given them their garb and rituals.

The five original military associations are the Fox, Elk (or Hoof Rattle), Shield, Dog, and Bow-string (or Contrary). In the nineteenth century, after the annihilation of all the Bow-strings by the Pawnees in 1837, Owl Man started a new warriors' club, the Wolf (or Owl Man's Bow-string), as the result of a vision experienced when starving and freezing on a journey north. The Northern Crazy Dogs is the seventh club, a contrary association also patterned on the Bow-string idea and undoubtedly influenced in part by the Crow Indian Crazy-Dogs-Wishing-to-Die (see Lowie 1935:331-334).

In many primitive cultures, especially in Africa and Melanesia, men's clubs are age graded. Although this is true of the warrior societies of the sedentary Village tribes of the northern Plains Indians, the societies of the Cheyennes, in common with the majority of Plains tribes, are ungraded. This means that the boys of a certain age do not join the lowest ranking club as a body and then progressively move up the ladder of clubs as they get older. When a Cheyenne boy is ready to go to war, he may join any club of his choosing; he may shift his membership later on, but it is most rare for him to do so. No one club is higher in status than another, although the popularity and prestige of the societies do shift from time to time. All the fraternities are fundamentally alike in their internal organization and activities; the differences are in their paraphernalia, dress, dances, and songs.

Each club has four officers or leaders. The leaders are the main war chiefs of the tribe, although any competent man may organize and lead a war party. The two head chiefs, who are the ritual leaders, sit at the back of the lodge when the club is meeting. The other two sit on either side of the door and serve as messengers—one might even say "ambassadors"—to the Council of Forty-four and the other military societies whenever a big issue is being discussed within the camp. These two are the bravest men in the society. They hold the post of honor at the door because when the camp is pitched tipi to tipi in expectation of an enemy attack, they hold the open gap in the circle against all assault.

Five of the seven associations also have four virgin daughters of tribal chiefs as maids of honor to participate in their ceremonies and to sit in the midst of the circle of war chiefs when they meet in common council. Select girls of "the very best families" who exemplify the Cheyenne ideal of chastity and perfect conduct are thus held up for others to emulate. Womanhood, though it is denied direct access to power and authority, receives high deference and social reward. All the members of a society call their four maids by the kin term "sister," and they may never marry one of their own maidens. Should one of these girls defile her chastity before she marries, it will bring bad luck to the warriors of her club. The Dog and Contrary Soldiers claim that they do not have any maids of honor because they do not dare to run the risk of the girls making a slip.

Two of the concise descriptions given by Dorsey provide a sample of the features that characterize the different societies.

The Elk (Hoof-Rattle) society has over . . . one hundred warriors . . . and four Cheyenne maidens. There is a keeper of the drums and a keeper of the elk antler emblem, which is formed like a rattlesnake. Two of the bravest men carry spears with crooks at one end, the wood of the handle being bent around in a semicircumference. These two spears are wrapped as far as the points with otter skin. The shaft is further ornamented with two bands of otter skin about two feet apart, with four pendants of eagle feathers attached to each band for ornamentation. The spears are about eight feet long. All of the other warriors carry straight spears with points, wrapped with otter skin which has been dressed on the outside. Each warrior carries a rattle. This rattle is a stick about one foot long, covered with tanned buckskin, to which are sewed or tied several dry dew-claws of elk, deer, or antelope. The keeper of the elk horn is the leader in the dancing and singing. The elk antler used by these warriors is real. It is straight and has a body about two inches thick and about eighteen inches long. It has a head and a tail. It is fashioned like a snake. On the top of the snake's back are grooves cut about half an inch apart. When used for singing and dancing they put one end of this antler snake on top of a piece of rawhide and hold the snake's tail in the left hand and with the right hand they hold the shin bone of an antelope and rub it backwards and forwards over the snake's back, thus producing a loud, shrill sound like that of some animal. They have four sacred songs, four war songs, and about two hundred dance songs. One hundred or more warriors sing in unison with the time of the rubbing on the elk antler, thus making themselves heard for a long distance. According to the teachings of the great Prophet this antler was used to charm the buffalo. Whenever the tribe desired large herds of buffalo, elk, or deer to come near their camp the warriors would come together and chew the herb medicine used in all the sacred arrow ceremonies and blow it upon the elk antler to make it effective. Then the keeper would hold the snake effigy by the tail and draw the scapula toward himself so that the motion was made from the head to the tail. Having four times made this motion the buffalo and deer would be charmed and come to them. All the antelope and deer thus affected were killed and their dew-claws taken for making rattles for the warriors.

Aside from the rattles, spears, bows and arrows, individuals satisfy their own desires in the matter of dress. All the warriors of the various societies hold as sacred the elk antler. When dancing, the Hoof-Rattlers hold their spears in one hand and their body erect. They jump up and down, keeping time with the singing and rattle.

The Fox or Coyote society derives its name from the fact that its members imitate the coyote in their power of endurance, cunning and activity. They outstrip their fellow-tribesmen in running long distances, playing games, etc. There are about one hundred and fifty warriors in this society, and a head chief, who carries a coyote hide with the hair left on. The society regards this hide as sacred. Having put their medicine on the coyote hide as well as on themselves, these warriors feel light, and can endure and can run a long distance without stopping. The society has a rattle keeper, who carries a red-painted gourd with stones inside to make the rattling. In old times this rattle was made out of buffalo hide, but lately the gourd has taken its place. This rattle is used to mark time in the dancing and singing, and its keeper is the leader in the dancing and singing, and he knows all the songs. The society has four sacred songs, part of which relate to the coyote; four war songs, and about three hundred dance songs.

When these warriors have a four days' dance they put up their lodge either in the center or in front of the camp-circle, and just within the interior of the lodge the coyote hide is placed so that its head is directed toward the entrance. The chief with his assistants sit back of the coyote hide. When in view, this coyote hide is placed in front of the chiefs in the council circle. The four maidens who are admitted to this society sit in front of the chiefs. Two of the warriors carry a spear about an inch and a half wide. Between its ends is stretched a string, which gives the spear the form of a bow. Several kinds of feathers hang from the spear, and it has a sharp point. The other warriors carry straight spears. Each warrior has two eagle feathers stuck vertically in his scalplock, and carries a bow and arrows. All members of the society dress alike. Their bodies and upper parts of their arms and legs are painted yellow, while the lower arms and legs are painted black. On the breast of each warrior, suspended by means of a string about the neck, is a crescent-shaped, black-painted piece of hide. The two eagle feathers in the hair are always worn and the spear is always carried in their hand when they are not abroad. When dancing these warriors jump up and down rapidly, keeping time to the rapid and ever-increasing time of the music. The four maidens, who are daughters of chiefs, decorate their dress with elk teeth. Their faces are painted yellow and they wear two eagle feathers upright in their hair.

In the past the warriors of this society had their hair roached over the top from front to back to represent a scalplock, the sides of the head being shorn of hair. All members of the other societies wore their hair long. The coyote hide is the emblem of this society, for in a similar skin the great Prophet brought the medicine-arrows to the tribe. The coyote was the animal that the great Spirit sent to wander over the earth, and he was one of the animals that, in early time, talked to men. (Dorsey 1905:I, 18-20) [Note: Dorsey substitutes fox for coyote because he obtained his information from Southern Cheyenne informants. In the south, the coyote was substituted for the fox during the nineteenth century.]

Several of the auxiliary activities of the military societies have already been noted—their policing of the great tribal ceremonies and the communal hunts, for instance, as well as such special activities as calling the buffalo and antelope. Their very important roles in government and law will be discussed in Chapter 5.

4

The Council of Forty-four

THE KEYSTONE of the Cheyenne social structure is the tribal council of forty-four peace chiefs. War may be a major concern of the Cheyennes and defense against the hostile Crow and Pawnee a major problem of survival, yet clearly the Cheyennes sense that a more fundamental problem is the danger of disintegration through internal dissension and aggressive impulses of Cheyenne against Cheyenne. Hence, the supreme authority of the tribe lies not in the hands of aggressive war leaders but under the control of even-tempered peace chiefs. All the peace chiefs are proven warriors, but when a chief of a military association is raised to the rank of peace chief, he must resign his post in the military society. He retains his membership, but not his position as war chief. The fundamental separation of civil and military powers, with the supremacy of the civil, which is characteristic of so many American Indian tribes and is written into the Constitution of the United States, is most explicit in the unwritten constitution of the Cheyenne nation.

A Cheyenne peace chief is chosen for a definite term of office—ten years—and ritually inducted as a member of the council. Each chief is a representative of his band and he is always a headman of an extended family. He is first and foremost, however, a "protector of the people," a "father" to each and every member of the tribe, and is addressed as such.

The personal requirements for a tribal chief, reiterated again and again by the Cheyennes, are an even-tempered good nature, energy, wisdom, kindliness, concern for the well-being of others, courage, generosity, and altruism. These traits express the epitome of the Cheyenne ideal personality. In specific behavior this means that a tribal chief gives constantly to the poor. "Whatever you ask of a chief, he gives it to you. If someone wants to borrow something of a chief, he gives it to that person outright."

"This is the first time since I have become a big [tribal] chief that I have happened upon such a poor man," announced High Backed Wolf after he had found Pawnee, who had been stripped and beaten by the Bow-string

Soldiers for his crimes: "now I am going to outfit him." "Now I am going to help you out," he addressed Pawnee, after giving him a stiff lecture on proper Cheyenne behavior. "That is what I am here for, because I am a chief of the people. Here are your clothes. Outside are three horses. You may take your choice! Here is a mountain lion skin. I used to wear this in the parades. Now I give it to you." To these things he also added a six-shooter. (Lewellyn and Hoebel 1941:8). Such is the conduct of a chief.

Where ordinary men customarily accept damages when their wives run off with another man, a tribal chief refuses the pipe, horse, and gifts sent by the correspondent; acceptance implies that he nourishes a grievance that must be salved. Instead, he summons his soldier society to his own lodge and ritually smokes his own pipe with them. Nothing is said about the matter, but everyone understands the chief to signify that the affair is formally closed.

When Arapaho Chief was having a scalp shirt made, word was brought to him that his wife had run off with another man. He merely filled his pipe and passed it to the other men, saying he had no fault to find with her. (It is also clear that his wife knew it was perfectly safe to run away—especially when such a sacred thing as a scalp shirt was occupying her husband.) Chiefs, when such an advantage is taken of them, sometimes show their superiority to the indignity by remarking most casually, "A dog has pissed on my tipi." Men who do not have faith in their ability to control their feelings under extreme provocation refuse to accept a chieftaincy. When Little Wolf indicated he intended to name Sun Road as his successor as the Sweet Medicine Chief, in 1892, Sun Road refused, saying, "When a dog is running after a bitch in heat —if my wife is chased by another man, I might weaken and open my mouth. Then it would be well if another had the medicine and not I."

As Grinnell sums it up,

> A good chief gave his whole heart and his whole mind to the work of helping his people, and strove for their welfare with an earnestness and a devotion rarely equaled by the rulers of other men. Such thought for his fellows was not without its influence on the man himself; after a time the spirit of goodwill which animated him became reflected in his countenance, so that as he grew old such a chief often came to have a most benevolent and kindly expression. Yet, though simple, honest, generous, tender-hearted, and often merry and jolly, when occasion demanded he could be stern, severe, and inflexible of purpose . . . . They were like the conventional notion of Indians in nothing save in the color of their skin. True friends, delightful companions, wise counselors, they were men whose attitude toward their fellows we might all emulate. (Grinnell 1923:I, 336-337)

Such is the stuff the responsible leaders of the Cheyenne people are made of.

The charter of the institution of chieftainship and its organization in the Council of Forty-four is sacred. Sweet Medicine gave the people the Sacred Arrows and many other customs and institutions; Erect Horns brought them the Sun Dance and Animal Dance by way of the Suhtai. But the mythological origin of the tribal council antedates all of these. Mooney (1907:371) cites a Cheyenne myth attributing the creation of the tribal council to a captive woman. Her husband had been a chief in her former tribe and she taught the Cheyennes its governmental organization. Grinnell (1923:I, 345) records a version in which a Cheyenne girl is taken captive by the Assiniboines. After a number of years she returns to the Cheyennes and tells them how the Assiniboines govern themselves; the Cheyennes, who are impressed with her account, adopt the Assiniboine system. The fact is, however, that the Assiniboines never had a tribal council anything like that of the Cheyennes.

The fullest recorded version of the origin myth of the Cheyenne Council of Forty-four is that recited to me by Black Wolf in 1936.

I once asked Elk River, when he was an old man, about that question. "Now we have chiefs," I said to him. "I wonder how we got those chiefs. Can you tell me? And how did we come to get the law against killing our own people?" This was many years ago and there were many people in the lodge when Elk River gave his reply.

"Yes," Elk River answered, "that was a long time ago, many years before our time, that this thing of which I shall tell took place."

This is what Elk River told. . .

People used to wander about the country in those days. There was one old man among them who took his family away from the main band to camp out alone. He stayed out here with them—his wife, his daughter, and a small son—for a long time, until one day he killed his wife and deserted his motherless children.

The orphan children wandered alone about the countryside seeking their tribesmen and shelter. At last they spied the main camp of their people in the distance. The first lodge they came to was that of an old woman of whom they asked news of their father. The old woman did not answer, but went to the lodge of an old man who was a camp crier to tell him that the children of Bull Looks Back had returned to the camp seeking after their father. This old man went out and announced the news to all the camp.

Bull Looks Back was right there among the people. When he heard the news he ran crying to the announcer, "Those monstrous children of mine killed their own mother out there and have eaten her flesh. That is why I left them. Tell the people that even though they are my own offspring, I say they should be staked to the ground and abandoned."

The camp crier repeated all that Bull Looks Back had said. "In the morning we must tie them to the ground and move camp as early as we can. We must not leave a living thing with them, not even dogs."

That night the people prepared green rawhide in rope lengths. The next morning they tied the boy and the girl to stakes driven in the ground and waited, sitting watching, until the thongs had shrunken tight and firm. Then the camp was moved.

[At this point the train of the narrative was broken when Black Wolf was asked whether a soldier society had carried out the deed. In response he gave the polite rebuke, "No, I asked Elk River that same question. 'I am telling the story,' he said. 'I'll come to that.' "]

There was one great, black dog. Maybe it had pups. At any rate, it had packed some stuff, meat and sinew, into a hole near the camp site. Toward evening the hapless siblings saw the dog coming up to them. It wriggled and scratched as a dog does and then went right to work chewing on the rope which bound the girl's wrists until they came free. The girl then untied her brother. They followed the dog to its hole in the creek bank, where it crawled in, and when it came out again it was dragging dried meat and some tools. They all ate and sat there.

During the night someone walked up to them, but the sister did not look up, for her head was hung in sorrow. This person addressed her little brother.

"Over there you will see a wikiup and an arbor. Go to it!"

"Sister," the little boy cried, "Look over there!"

"It will do me no good to look," she murmured. "They have been telling lies about us. This person has not come here to speak the truth."

"Look anyhow," the boy insisted.

So she raised her head, and she saw it was true.

Then the stranger spoke again. "In the morning—at daylight—a herd of buffalo will come. Have your sister look at them."

At daylight the buffalo came as the stranger had said. "My sister, look on those buffalo," the boy cried in delight.

"That herd won't die if I do look at them," she morosely replied.

Even so, she had medicine power from the man who had been there, though she did not know it. She looked, and at her glance all the buffalo fell dead! After that the boy and girl went to the wikiup.

A bear and a mountain lion were living there. Three beds were made up in the hut, so the boy and girl took the extra one.

Again the strange visitor appeared before the outcasts. He spoke to the boy as before. "Tell your sister she must butcher all those buffalo. She must look after all the meat and take care of all the fat. A big crow will come to one of these trees. When she has done her butchering she must put some kidney fat in the branches for it. That will be on the third day."

In the end, when the girl had finished her butchering, a crow flew down and looked at them. The sister spoke to it, because she now believed in the stranger. "Here, come get this fat. Fly with it straight to our people's camp. Fly right through the opening [in the camp circle]. Fly low about the circle. Then drop this in the center before the lodges. Tell those people it is from the children they left on the prairie to die."

When the people saw this, and understood the crow to mean that the two children had plenty of meat, they made ready to move the camp back to them, because they had been unable to find game for some time.

The boy and girl heard a man come singing. He was singing Elk songs.

"That is my father," the girl told the lion and the bear. "Do not harm him until he has eaten, but when he leaves this lodge, take him."

When the father came in, he was given the place at the back of the lodge. The girl sent word to the approaching people not to move in too close to her.

"I shall see you tomorrow," was her order.

When her father finished eating, the lion and the bear killed him for her.

She now sent for the men, and the women too, because she had cooked up a lot of food. When they had eaten she spoke to the men.

"Tomorrow you move down on this flat and put yourselves in a nice circle. We are going to make chiefs. You people know I have been accused of killing my mother. That is not true. Now, however, I have killed my father through animals. We shall make chiefs, and hereafter we shall make a rule that if anyone kills a fellow tribesman he shall be ordered out of the camp for from one to five years. Whatever the people decide."

When they had arranged the camp circle they took two big lodges and made one in the center. She asked them to move five other tipis into the space within the circle. These were put in the medicine wheel arrangment. When everything was finished she packed a large bundle and walked around the circle to enter it before the big lodge. First, she took some dirt from the north side of the lodge. Carefully patting it she arranged it in a mound in the center of a cleared space. It represented the world. Next she set up five sticks representing the men she would choose as head chiefs. She filled her pipe. She held it to each stick, showing the people what would be expected of them.

"You will have to swear," she said. "You will have to take an oath that you will be honest and care for all the tribe."

Following the instructions she gave out, her brother purified himself in the smudge of the sweet medicine grass. Now she told him to go out to walk four times around the camp.

"When you go out you have a starting place. Go around until you come back to it. Do this four times," she ordered.

He had already been told what men to select. After the four circum-ambulations he sought out the first man, leading him into the lodge. Then the other four were brought in like manner.

When they were seated the sister told them everything. She had all she needed in that bundle. She told them she was going to make them chiefs to rule the camp. And this is what she said.

"You have seen me put up five sticks here. You shall have to do this to the others who come after you. Now you five men are to be the chiefs of the entire tribe. You must rule the people. When the tribe comes to renew the chiefs you must put up these five sticks again. If anyone of you still lives, and the people want him again, then you must call him in to take his old place."

Now she has finished telling them. [Changes of tense are the narrator's.] She is going to swear them in. She is holding the pipe herself, in both hands with the stem out. They smoked. The pipe is smoked for peace. That was done so that if some persons ever used strong words to the chiefs, they would have strong hearts and not get angry. The sweet grass was used on all of them.

Then the big crowd came in. Enough more were in the lodge to make forty-four men. She did the same to each of the rest of them. When this was done she told them to pick two men to sit on each side of the entrance.

"Some day you will have a lodge of your own," she informed them. "Then you can use these two. They can cook for you, or you can send them out on errands. They shall be your servants and messengers."

These two could not be of the five.

"Every ten years you must renew the chiefs. But each time keep five of the old ones," the maid continued.

She had a parfleche for the stuff they used in the ritual.

"When you move camp," she exhorted them in closing, "keep out in front of the people. Stop and rest four times with it [the chiefs' bundle] on the way." (Llewellyn and Hoebel 1941: 69-73)

After she had made all the chiefs, she took out five bones, just as many as these five chiefs. "Now you can make soldiers troops. You may call them what you want. You could call one Elks." Later on, Sweet Medicine made the dress of the soldiers.

"When you people move camp, leave me here. Every four years, you come back to this place where I will be."

Next she made a medicine wheel and a buffalo horn which she gave to the old woman to whose lodge she had first come. "On your travels you will sometimes go hungry. If you use these, it will make the chiefs think of their duty."

Later that year the people were hungry. Then the old woman remembered what had been told her. She told a young man she was going to try it out. She had him go collect some rose berries. She cooked them up. That night she had him stay in her lodge to help her. They built an incense smudge of cedar and coals over which they purified her pipe, wheel, and buffalo horn. She sang four holy songs all through. When each was done, she ritually smoked the pipe. Then it was daylight.

She told the boy to go up a hill to scout. "We shall see if she told us the truth."

From the top of the hill he spied buffalo in the distance. He came back and reported the news.

"Good," she said. "Go get Howling Wolf." He was one of the new door chiefs.

Howling Wolf sent out a crier to tell the people, and they went out on the hunt right from the camp, the buffalo were so close.

After they had the hunt and everyone had his meat, they asked the boy how he knew there were buffalo out there; they had not seen any for several days.

"My grandmother did that," he told them. "She fixed up her lodge and did the ceremony the way that girl told her. The woman we left behind in her camp and were not to see until next fall, she had the power to do this."

After that, a bunch of chiefs went into the old woman, asking her how she knew the buffalo were going to be there that morning.

She replied, "I was told how to do this by the girl who was left behind in camp. She told me how to do it. I am only supposed to do this once in a while when there is great need. If you chiefs will fill up the pipe and bring it in here, I'll tell you how to do it. Take out the tenderloin from a buffalo. Dry it well. Pound it up very fine. Keep this handy."

The camp had been moving for some time; they were running out of food again. One of the chiefs asked the young man to ask his grandmother if it would be the right time to ask for more food. His grandmother told him, "Tell the chiefs to come to my lodge late this evening just before sunset. All who are coming must enter at the same time." She told him what they must bring—that tenderloin powder, rose haws, and pomme blanche (prairie potato). When they got there, the pipe was the first to go in. She had the lodge all fixed; the Earth and everything were ready.

One of the chiefs did the speaking, begging her to show them how her power went. The old woman told them, "I am not the one who is doing this. I am only performing as *she* told me. She sent us out on the move to keep going until fall. When we get back to her camp, my job is done. I am teaching you this now in case anything might happen to me!"

They laid out the horn. Then she took the pipe, pointing it in the five directions. They smoked.

Then she spoke, "I am not supposed to do this as long as there is a single buffalo for the hunters to take. I could not do this on my own. This is not just my doings. It is given to me to do for the people."

She then made the remark, "I'll still use this young man as my helper."

"Bring me a coal and place it here."

On this she put some sweet grass.

"Now I am going to sing four songs. At the end, we shall smoke. You chiefs have the pipe ready before me."

She sang the first song and then lit the pipe, praying as she pointed it to the five directions. When all had smoked, the boy had to get a fresh coal.

They refilled the pipe, and she sang the second song. At the end, all smoked again.

They did this for each song. It took them all night. Daylight was breaking as the old woman finished the fourth song.

When the song was done, she addressed them, "Now that grandson of mine, my helper; he usually does these things for me, but you chiefs, you are the ones who want to know how this is done. Is there any young man among you who is willing to go out and see?"

Howling Wolf was in there. He was the one they chose.

She spoke to Howling Wolf as follows, "Now I want you to do just as my grandson has done. Get a coal and put it before me with the sweet grass!"

She smoked all those ritual things in the incense. The last thing was done. The ceremony was finished. She was talking all the time to this man, instructing him. "When you go out the tipi door, turn south and then go west. When you see the buffalo, keep going and turn back; come in the north side of the lodge."

He made his trip quite aways out. He came back and reported buffalo moving toward the camp making quite a noise. The chiefs sent him right out to tell the same old man to cry the news to the whole camp. When it was announced, all the men got ready for the hunt. After the chase, they all came back with meat. They just had all the meat they could handle.

It was announced through the camp that they were going to help the old woman out. They all thought that she was a great woman—a medicine woman. They brought her meat and clothes.

Then they started back to find the holy girl who had given them these things. It was fall when they got there. She told her little brother to tell the chiefs to arrange the camp in a circle as before. The old woman and her helper seemed to be the only two would could go into the girl's lodge. The girl told her, "Now when you go back to the camp, tell the people they must put up a dance. They must build a great skunk (bonfire). One bunch of solders must dance. Then another, until all have danced."

The soldiers were going to select one of the chiefs to be out in front. Certain persons were selected to do the choosing. Four men from each soldier society and four from the council of chiefs were chosen. When the warriors were all in line with these men out in front, this holy woman emerged from her lodge, standing before them.

She spoke to the four chiefs, "These men your warriors have selected are your soldier chiefs. You must now fill your pipe and swear them in. They are here to protect you. You are to look out for the people. When there is fighting or work to be done, these soldier chiefs are here to do it."

"Now you may wander about the country again, wherever you wish to go. But do not forget this one thing, ever. Every now and then repeat this ceremony. Your four head chiefs are to remind the soldier chiefs of their duty."

"And never come back to this spot again. I shall leave here and you shall never more see me. And another thing, do not abuse the dog. It was the dog who saved my life and taught me these things."

"In your wanderings, the time will come when you will meet a great holy man [Sweet Medicine]. He will change your way of life. He will tell you where to go. He will give you your home."

"My brother and I will leave this earth. We may go up into the heavens. Yet I shall always be working for the people. I may be a star." Her name was Mukije, Short Woman.

Thus ended the story as told by Elk River, who was born about 1810 and died in 1908 (Hoebel n.d.).

There are a number of aspects to this myth. First, it establishes the tribal council as supernaturally vested and as the oldest of the existing institutions of the formal social structure, thus the ultimate authority. Second, the act of perfidy and abuse of children by a parent, and the killing of the parent in revenge are examples of what may happen within the society if there are no strong regulations to prevent it—an anarchy the Cheyennes feel must ever be guarded against. Third, in times of personal stress and despair, supernatural animals appear to give power and instruction in how to achieve one's goals. Fourth, the military societies were given their governmental functions after the tribal council was formed and are explicitly made subordinate to the council in these matters. Fifth, it is made clear that Sweet Medicine and his innovations are a later event in Cheyenne mythological history. Sixth, ritual acts have a compulsive effect in producing desired results.

Let us now turn to the actual organization of the council. Its presiding officer, the head priest-chief of the tribe, is the Sweet Medicine Chief. He holds the Sweet Medicine Bundle, a small ritual package of sweet grass passed from one office holder to the next. He is taught the rituals of his office by his predecessor. When the council is in session, he sits at the west side of the Chief's

Lodge. The spot at which he sits is called "the center of the universe," *heum* (the zenith, the above), and this is the title the Sweet Medicine Chief carries. In front of him, in the lodge floor, is the usual smoothed-out circle of earth, representing the world. Around it are placed, upright in the ground, the five sticks representing the five medicine chiefs, Heum and his four associates.

These four also represent cosmic spiritual beings, and each of them must have pledged or acted as instructor in either the Arrow Renewal, Crazy Animal Dance, or Sun Dance at least four times. The one who sits in the southeast side of the lodge circle is called *hunsowun* (an untranslatable holy name). He represents the Spirit Who Rules the Summer. He is always an Animal Dance priest. Across from him, in the northeast position, sits the representative of the *maijunemistist* (the Big Holy People—those who know everything, those who taught Sweet Medicine and Erect Horns; they are associated with the Northern Lights). This direction and its associated chief is also called *maxkeometaneo* (Where the Food Comes From). In the southwest position sits *niomataneo* (an untranslatable holy name), who is associated with *aijunt'tsemiatsse* (the Spirit Who Rules the Ages). He is always a Wolf Cub Ceremony priest. Opposite him, at the northwestern spot, sits the *no'tam* (another untranslatable holy name), who represents *paiwustannewuste* (the Spirit Who Gives Good Health).

The mystic symbolism of the dependence of the Cheyenne on the supernatural world is thus woven into the very nucleus of their governmental structure. At its heart, in their belief, the council is not just a body of their wisest men, but a council of men in empathy with the spiritual forces that dominate all life—beneficent forces from which come all good things the Cheyenne heart desires, forces that respond to their hopes and needs so long as the compulsive ritual acts are faithfully repeated.

The five sacred chiefs are always chosen from among those who have already served a full term of office as an ordinary chief. A sacred chief may succeed himself for a second term, or he may step down to an ordina_y chieftainship if he feels he does not want to carry the responsibility of the office any longer. At the end of his term as one of the five, Brave Wolf got up and told the other chiefs how he had served the people as chief, how he had been through many ceremonies for them, how he now wanted to be relieved. They agreed, but "held him in the lodge"—that is, named him to one of the thirty-nine lesser positions. Under no circumstances may a tribal chief be impeached or deposed during his ten-year tenure of office, not even for murder. When Little Wolf killed Starving Elk in 1879 (see Llewellyn and Hoebel 1941: 82-84 for the details of the case) he was then the Sweet Medicine Chief. Although he went into exile, he still remained chief, and when the council convened for the next renewal it could not proceed until Little Wolf had been induced to come in and officiate over the rituals. "I've done wrong," he told them. "I killed a man, and I don't think I ought to sit with the chiefs."

"We need you," was the council's reply. "We can't proceed without you." But he was not retained as a member of the council. Grasshopper replaced him as the last head chief of the Cheyennes. When Grasshopper died, the

Sweet Medicine Bundle was gone. The Cheyennes believed it had been contaminated by contact with Little Wolf's body, and so Grasshopper buried it.

A hundred years earlier, before 1800, another chief had killed a tribesman and was banished. People talked against him, saying, "We will take him out of his place." "But," in the words of Calf Woman, "the Indian law stopped it . . . he was still a chief, though all by himself." After two years, he was allowed to rejoin the tribe and resume his functions as a chief.

Bear Runs Out, as a young chief, accepted a horse as damages from a young man he had seen flirting with his wife. For this unchiefly conduct he was censured, and when his term was up, he was let out of the council. After another ten-year term had passed, and he was a mature man of more sober judgment, he was renamed to the council because "he was a great protector of the people in war."

Each chief, if he is still alive at the end of his term, chooses his own successor from within his own band. Thus every band normally has at least four representatives on the council. Although the office is not hereditary, a man frequently chooses his own son to succeed him—if the son measures up to the qualification for chieftainship. The office is always looked upon as a grave responsibility and not as a political plum. It brings respect and honor, but nothing else. There are no economic advantages; quite to the contrary, being a chief means having a drain on one's resources. "Among those qualified for the position of chief, there was no strife as to who should secure it, no 'wire-pulling' or intrigue" (Grinnell 1923:I, 341). Refusal to accept a nomination brings bad luck. Big Head, for example, refused a chieftainship in the middle of the last century. He was killed in his next battle.

The Chiefs' •Renewal, or the naming and investiture of a new council, is almost as solemn and important a ritual undertaking as the Medicine Arrow Renewal. The Chiefs' Lodge is placed in the center of the camp circle, with the Arrow Keeper's and Buffalo Hat Keeper's lodges also in the open space within the circle. Four days of secret world-revitalization rites precede the actual selection and investiture of the new council. At the end, each new chief gives his predecessor a gift. All the chiefs come forth to be viewed by the people, and the ceremony is followed by festive feasts in honor of the chiefs and the giving of many presents by the new chiefs, especially to poor people.

Cheyenne government, it may be seen, is highly democratic and representative of the people's concerns. Each band has an approximately equal number of members on the council, and the ratio of forty-four chiefs for no more than four thousand Cheyennes is better than one representative to one hundred citizens.

The council is a serenely deliberative body. As described by Grinnell,

> At the meetings of the council of chiefs, questions of interest to the tribe were considered. Concerning minor matters, one of the principal chiefs was likely to express his opinion, and, if supported by another principal chief, the council assented without debate. Questions of greater importance, such as moving the camp when buffalo could not be found, of undertaking a tribal war, or of seeking an alliance with other tribes for

the purpose of proceeding to war against a common enemy, were discussed at great length, the deliberations perhaps extending over several meetings. In such debates the talking was done chiefly by the older men—those of greatest experience—yet after the elders had expressed their views, middle-aged men expressed theirs, and even younger men might speak a few words, suggesting a different point of view, or giving new reasons for or against a certain course.

Such councils were conducted with much form and with a degree of courtesy that could hardly be exceeded. Usually the subject of the council was known in advance and to some extent had been discussed. When all the chiefs were present, a few minutes of silence ensued, then one of the older men arose and introduced the subject at issue. His remarks were followed by a brief silence for consideration, when another old man followed him and the discussion continued. Sometimes there were wide differences of opinion among the men, yet each was listened to gravely and with respect, and no matter how earnest the debate might become, no man ever interrupted a speaker, nor did anything like wrangling occur. (Grinnell 1923:I, 338-339)

Although only the chiefs themselves and a few other older men may be in the lodge, most such meetings take place in the summer when the tipi sides are rolled up, and a large public audience sits around outside listening to the discussions. As soon as a decision is reached, a camp crier rides through the camp circle announcing the decision of the council. The chiefs discuss the reasons for the action with their own kindred and bands, so that everyone is well informed as to what is to be done—and why.

In addition to treating of such matters as camp moving and tribal (as against individual raiding expeditions) war policy, the council also acts as a judicial body in cases involving a criminal act (see Chapter 5). In governmental affairs, it further serves as executive and legislative authority over the military societies, which act as the administrative police branch. In matters of war and peace, however, the warrior groups have an active say in the decision-making process. They can, in fact, ignore and thereby nullify the ruling of the council in matters in which they are vitally concerned. The council, although it has the constitutional authority to act on its own, takes realistic cognizance of this hard fact.

Thus when the Kiowas and Comanches, hereditary enemies of the Cheyennes, made a proffer of peace to Seven Bulls and his war party of eight men (they were brought together by an Arapaho host in whose camp the Cheyennes and their enemies accidentally came together as guests), Seven Bulls replied,

Friend, you know we are not chiefs. We cannot smoke with these men, nor make peace with them. We have no authority; we can only carry the message. I have listened to what you say and tomorrow with my party I will start back to our Cheyenne village, and will carry this word to our chiefs. They must decide what shall be done. We are young men; we cannot say anything; but we will take your message back to the chiefs.

He was as good as his word. The council was assembled the day after his return and he and his companions were invited in to report their message. Prolonged debate brought no agreement. Then the proposal was made to put the question to the Dog Soldiers. This was accepted and the two Door Chiefs of the Dog Soldiers, White Antelope and Little Old Man, were sent for. After a briefing, High Backed Wolf, the presiding officer of the council, told them, "Now, my friends, you go and assemble your Dog Soldiers. Tell them about this matter and talk it over among them. Let us know what you think of it. Tell us what you think is best to be done."

When the Dog Soldiers had convened in their lodge, White Antelope described the problem in full, concluding his remarks with, "The chiefs are leaving this matter to us, because we are the strongest of the military groups. It is my own thoughts that our chiefs are in favor of making peace. What do you all think about it?"

The Dogs unanimously agreed to leave the decision to White Antelope and Little Old Man, who were their two bravest leaders.

They declared for peace with the Kiowas and Comanches. On their return to the Council Lodge, this was the decision they recommended on behalf of the Dogs. Thereupon, the chiefs all arose and thanked them gravely. This done, they sent the crier about the camp to announce that the council had decided peace would be made with their erstwhile enemies (Grinnell 1915: 60-66). Thus began in 1840 an alliance of friendship that was never violated. The matter began with the good offices of a third party, the Arapaho, and was carried with due respect for authority to the council. The council licked the thorny problem of possible defiance of its authority by delegating the power to act to the key group in question. The Dogs responded by recognizing the validity of the chiefs' inclinations. The Dogs forestalled dissension by delegating the decision to their two greatest warriors and then announced it to the council as a unanimous opinion. The council discharged the Dog Soldiers with thanks and asserted its paramount authority in announcing the decision as its own. Here is true parliamentary statecraft, a formal structure kept functionally flexible so that the structure remains intact and yet expediently gives when necessary to achieve an important immediate goal not otherwise likely to be realized.

5

Law and Justice

L AW MAY OR MAY NOT be a matter of government, although it is always
a matter of political organization—the system of regulation of relations between groups or members of different groups within the society
at large. Public law—the body of legal rules governing conduct held to be of
such concern to the whole society that it is administered by public officials in
the name of, and on behalf of, the society as an entity—is an aspect of government. Private law—the body of legal rules governing conduct deemed to be
of immediate concern to the injured party but indirectly recognized as of
concern to the society at large—although not necessarily an aspect of government, is always an important part of political organization. In many primitive law systems, private law predominates over public law; not so, in the case
of the Cheyennes.

The Cheyenne concern with the threat of internal disruption and their
compensatory drive toward tribal supremacy and unity on all crucial matters
have resulted in the centralization of legal control in the tribal council and the
military societies. The bulk of Cheyenne law is public law: the heart of Cheyenne law focuses on murder and the control of the communal hunt; disputes
over property are rare, adultery and wife stealing rarer. Violence of Cheyenne
against Cheyenne is the great challenge to the Cheyenne system of social control, and the existence of this danger stems from the fact that Cheyenne basic
values are contradictory at certain points. On the one hand, the individual is
trained and encouraged to be militarily aggressive. He is publicly rewarded
with many ego-satisfying reinforcements for sterling performance on the battlefield. But—as will be demonstrated in Chapter 9—his training leads to strong
repression in the development of many phases of his personality. He is taught
to be competitive in the achievement of war status and horse-stealing repu-
tation. At the same time, he must repressively control his sex drives, and he
is trained in social altruism and mild demeanor within the camp. It is therefore not surprising that violent emotions often break through the bonds of

self-restraint in homicidal assaults on fellow tribesmen. In our special study of Cheyenne law (Llewellyn and Hoebel 1941) we obtained case records of sixteen intratribal killings over the four decades from 1835 to 1879.

As an operating system, Cheyenne law is remarkable for the degree of juristic skill that is manifest in it. By juristic skill we mean the creation and utilization of legal forms and processes that efficiently and effectively solve the problems posed to the law and in such a way that the basic values and purposes of the society are realized and not frustrated by rigid legalism. Juristic skill implies the ability to define relations between persons, to allocate authority, and to clear up conflicts of interests (trouble cases) in ways that effectively reduce internal social tensions and promote individual well-being and the maintenance of the group as a group. We have commented on this outstanding quality of the Cheyennes: "It is not merely that we find neat juristic work. It is that the *generality* of the Cheyennes, not alone the 'lawyers' or the 'great lawyers' among them (whom they show no signs of having recognized as such) worked out their nice cases with an intuitive juristic precision which among us marks a judge as good; that the *generality* among them produced indeed a large percentage of work on a level of which our rarer and greater jurists could be proud" (Llewellyn and Hoebel 1941:312-313).

The greatest of Cheyenne governmental and legal achievements has been the absolute and total elimination of feud. The feudistic tendency is the bane of primitive social systems generally. Feud means internal war, civil strife between the kinship groups within the society; feud means either the absence of law, or else the breakdown of legal machinery. The absence of feud among the Cheyenne is in part a result of the system of bilateral kindreds at the bottom of the social structure. In such a system the strands of kinship are generally diffused throughout the society in a more multiple way than is the case in unilaterally organized social structures. This factor, however, is not in itself a wholly efficient cause for the absence of feuding, for other bilateral societies are known to be plagued by feud. What, then, are the additional elements that have been worked into their culture by the Cheyennes?

We are already familiar with the ritual devices used to emphasize tribal unity and the importance of "Cheyenneness" above band identity. We have seen, further, how it is impressed upon the chiefs that denegation of self-interest is in harmony with a sense of obligation to the well-being of all the tribe. This emphasis, too, contributes to the reduction of the feud potential. But, in addition, there are specific concepts related to the killing of a fellow tribesman and specific mechanisms for dealing with homicide when it does occur.

The first of these is purely mystic and relates to the major tribal fetish, the Four Sacred Arrows. A murderer becomes personally polluted, and specks of blood contaminate the feathers of the Arrows. The very word for murder is *he'joxones,* "putrid." A Cheyenne who kills a fellow Cheyenne rots internally. His body gives off a fetid odor, a symbolic stigma of personal disintegration, which contrition may stay, but for which there is no cure. The smell is offensive to other Cheyennes, who will never again take food from a bowl used by the killer. Nor will they smoke a pipe that has touched his lips. They fear personal contamination with his "leprous" affliction. This means that the person who has become so un-Cheyenne as to fly in the face of the greatest of Cheyenne injunctions is cut off from participation in the symbolic acts of mutuality—eating from a common bowl and smoking the ritual pipe. With this alienation goes the loss of many civil privileges and the cooperative assistance of one's fellows outside of one's own family. The basic penalty for murder is therefore a lifetime of partial social ostracism.

On the legal level, the ostracism takes the form of immediate exile imposed by the Tribal Council sitting as a judicial body. The sentence of exile is enforced, if need be, by the military societies. The rationalization of the banishment is that the murder's stink is noisome to the buffalo. As long as an unatoned murderer is with the tribe, "game shuns the territory; it makes the tribe lonesome." Therefore, the murderer must leave.

Banishment is not in itself enough, however. His act has disrupted the fabric of tribal life. Symbolically, this is expressed in the soiling of the Arrows, the allegorical identity of the tribe itself. As long as the Arrows remain polluted, bad luck is believed to dog the tribe. Not only does the spectre of starvation threaten, but there can be no success in war or any other enterprise. The earth is disjointed and the tribe out of harmony with it. The Arrow Renewal is the means of righting the situation. The oneness of the tribe is reasserted in the required presence at the ceremony of every family—save those of murderers. The renewed earth, effected by the rites in the Lone Tipi, is fresh and unsullied, once again free of the stain of killing.

Such a concept of the effect of homicide within the tribe completely precludes the possibility of feud. Feud would merely compound the sin, making disaster for the tribe complete. Nor is there any possibility of a death penalty for the crime. Extrusion and ostracism are eminently effective. In the same vein, no steps are taken to compensate the bereaved kin group for the death of its member. The offense is against the well-being of all the people; hence concern of a mere kinship group is as nothing.

Yet it is contrary to Cheyenne principles to so ostracize a man forever. The Cheyennes cherish the individual personality. They value individualism, asking only that the individual never place himself above the tribal interest. They therefore work always toward reform and individual rehabilitation. For them, the law is corrective; it is never employed as a vindictively punitive measure. Punishment, in their view, need go no further than is necessary to make the individual see the right. Once they are convinced the knave is reformed, they move smoothly to reincorporate him into the community. The case of Pawnee, cited above, is but one example of this. So, also, with the murderer. After a period of years—three, five, or ten—his banishment may be commuted. At this point the feelings of the relatives of his victim are taken into consideration, for they must consent to the commutation.

For example: Cries Yia Eya was banished for killing Chief Eagle in a drunken brawl. He had not been seen for three years, when he turned up with a horse laden with tobacco. Stopping outside the camp, he had a friend lead the horse in to the chiefs along with the message, "I am begging to come home."

The chiefs called in the soldier chiefs and divided the tobacco among them, saying, "Now we want you soldiers to decide if you think we should accept his request. If you decide that we should let him return, then it is up to you to convince his family that it is all right."

The soldier chiefs convened their societies in their separate lodges. The door servants kept passing back and forth between them, reporting the trend of opinion. At last one man proposed, "I think it is all right. I believe the stink has blown from him. Let him return!" This view won out.

Then the father of Chief Eagle was sent for. "Soldiers," he replied, "I shall listen to you. Let him return! But if that man comes back, I want never to hear his voice raised against another person. If he does, we come together."

Cries Yia Eya, according to Calf Woman, had always been a mean, unpopular person, but after he came back to the camp he was always good to the people (Llewellyn and Hoebel 1941:12-13).

In one tragic incident, recorded by Grinnell, there was no reconciliation; rather, a tribal "execution" of a two-time killer was engineered. This case of a murderer irretrievably beyond the pale began in 1854, when Walking Coyote killed a chief of the Fox Soldiers, White Horse, for taking his wife. He had some cause for his extreme action in that White Horse had not sent him the customary pipe and gift. Another Cheyenne, called Winnebago, pledged the Arrow Renewal, but then overreached himself by preempting the wife that White Horse had originally taken. Walking Coyote retaliated by forcibly taking one of Winnebago's other wives while her husband was away in the north. Upon his return, Winnebago shot and killed Walking Coyote within his lodge.

The Arrows were renewed, and Winnebago left the tribe. But eight years later, he was back again when a kinsman of White Horse raised a dispute with him over ownership of a horse. In the brawling that followed, he killed this kinsman in self-defense. The Arrows were renewed again, and Winnebago went to live with the Arapahos.

Rising Fire, a member of the same kindred as Winnebago's two victims, was goaded into a grudge feeling against Winnebago by skillfully planted, malicious gossip. Winnebago was lured into an ambush by the members of his own Dog Society, who, inviting him into the Cheyenne camp for a feast, led him past the lodge of Rising Sun, who shot and killed him (Grinnell 1923:I, 350-353).

This case shows that residual urges to kin blood revenge are still present; that woman stealing, with arrogance, can occur—and is so outrageous in the view of the individual Cheyenne as to lead to utterly reckless behavior. And finally, that when banishment does not effect reformation (even though Winnebago was sorely provoked in his second killing), banishment is not enough; the death penalty can be imposed, but indirectly and by crafty expediency on the part of the soldiers. For there are no formal institutional patterns in Cheyenne culture to deal with this kind of marginal irresponsibility. It happened only once in all known Cheyenne history.

Suicide is homicide—a self-killing. We have already seen how brothers plan to get themselves killed when sisters flaunt their authority. But they let the enemy do the killing and their post-mortem reward is glory, not disapproval. Direct suicide is a protest act of girls and women, and for both, the protest is an expression of grievance within the conjugal family. The social reaction follows two lines. A woman who hangs herself because her husband brings home a second wife is said to be foolish for killing herself over such a little thing. Second wives are normal. In the public view there is no valid protest, and nothing is done about it. However, in two cases in which mothers abused and beat their daughters who then committed suicide (one for eloping with a boy of a family she disapproved of, the other for leaving her husband and joining in a young people's dance), the social reaction was quite otherwise. The women were publicly mobbed and then exiled. In both cases the Arrows were renewed (Llewellyn and Hoebel 1941:160-161).

Beating a child is considered violent intratribal aggression and is absolutely abhorred. The child reacts in extreme protest, thus placing on the parent the terrible onus of being "un-Cheyenne." The public finds an excuse to release its own pent-up aggressions in a violent but nonlethal outburst. The law then takes over.

Outrageous conduct leading to a protest suicide *is* tantamount to killing that person. Such conduct is *de jure* homicide. Banishment and tribal expiation must follow.

Abortion, too, is homicide within the meaning of Cheyenne law. An unborn fetus has legal personality as a Cheyenne. Its death through abortion brings the full penalty on its mother (Llewellyn and Hoebel 1941:118-119).

If the first concern of Cheyenne law is to nullify the dangers in intratribal killing, the second is to insure the security of the basic food supply through the communal hunt. From the time of the performance of the great ceremonies to the splitting up of the tribe at the end of the summer, no man or private group of men may hunt alone. During the summer months the bison are gathered in massive herds, but distances between herds may be great. A single hunter can stampede thousands of bison and spoil the hunt for the whole tribe. To prevent this, the rules are clear, activity is rigidly policed, and violations are summarily and vigorously punished. The police for any given summer are ordinarily the members of the soldier society of the pledger of the tribal ritual with which the summer has opened. If for any reason there is a question as to who should police the hunt, the Council of Forty-four names the fraternity which is to have the job.

In a typical case the tribe was moving up the Rosebud River in Montana looking for buffalo in the direction of the Big Horn Mountains. All the hunters were in a line with the Shield Soldiers to restrain them until the signal was given, for the scouts had reported buffalo. Just as the line came over a protecting ridge down wind from the buffalo, two men were seen riding in among the herd. At an order from their chief, the Shield Soldiers charged down on them. Little Old Man shouted that any who failed or hesitated to beat the miscreants would be beaten themselves. The first to reach the spot killed the two hunters' horses. As each soldier reached the criminals, he slashed them with his whip. Their guns were smashed.

The offenders were sons of a Dakota who had been living with the Cheyennes for some time. He said to his sons, "Now you have done wrong. You failed to obey the law of this tribe. You went out alone and you did not give the other people a chance."

The Shield Soldier chiefs took up the lecturing. The boys did not try to defend themselves, so the chiefs relented. They called on their men to consider the plight of the two delinquents, without horses or weapons. "What do you men want to do about it?" Two offered to give them horses. A third gave them two guns. All the others said, "Good!"

Then it was noticed that five or six members of the troop were not present. They were searched for and spotted chasing buffalo. A chief gave the order to charge and whip them but not to kill their horses. Big Footed Bull, who was one of the slackers, saw them coming. He took off his Hudson Bay blanket and spread it on the ground before his companions and himself. The soldiers rode around them in two columns, dismounted, and cut the blankets into strips to wear as part of their dance costumes. They did not whip the men, but they did cut an ear off each of their horses (Llewellyn and Hoebel 1941: 112-113).

In good Cheyenne manner, the first violators were severely punished—and then immediately rehabilitated as soon as the soldiers sensed they had learned their lesson. As for their duty-shirking comrades, they, too, quickly signalized their error by offering the blanket. They were spared physical punishment but their one-eared horses and the spectacle of the other members of their troop dancing with their blanket strips was an unpleasant public reminder for a long time to come.

Even the tipi of a person suspected of secretly hunting may be searched by the soldiers. Man-Lying-On-His-Back-With-His-Legs-Flexed accidently came upon a herd when the no-hunting rule was in force. He killed and butchered just one cow. He was seen and informed on. The Shield Soldiers went to his lodge and cut a gash down the back of it. He sat inside, saying nothing. By this they knew he was guilty, whereupon his whole lodge was destroyed. On another occasion, someone carried tales on Low Forehead. He was innocent, and rushed out holding up his hands in protest when the Fox Soldiers arrived at his lodge. Their chiefs entered and searched it. Finding nothing, they left him unmolested.

Such great tribal figures as Little Wolf and Old Bear have received punishment in their time for violating the hunting rules. On this one point the Cheyennes are most inflexible.

A special problem case was once raised in this connection by Sticks-Everything-Under-His-Belt. He announced ahead of time that he was going out hunting for himself. A special council of the Forty-four and all the military societies was called to deal with this crisis, for Sticks-Everything-Under-His-Belt had made it clear that he meant to act as though he were not a member of the tribe. The formal ruling was: So be it. No one might help him thereafter in any way. All the privileges of being a Cheyenne were to be denied him. But, the chiefs left the door open for his return. If anyone did help him, that person would have to give a Sun Dance. This was posed as a penalty. But giving a Sun Dance is an honor and, as we have seen, an occasion of tribal integration.

Sticks-Everything-Under-His-Belt went into mourning all alone. He was strictly shunned for several years. In the end, his sister's husband announced to the chiefs that he was bringing him back into the tribe, if the chiefs would agree. They thanked him, saying, "We are very glad you are going to bring back this man. However, let him remember that he will be bound by whatever rules the soldiers lay down for the tribe. He may not say he is outside of them. He has been out of the tribe for a long time. If he remembers these things, he may come back."

Then Sticks-Everything-Under-His-Belt was invited to appear before the council. The pipe was passed and smoked by all. Then he declared himself. "From now on," he asseverated, "I am going to run with the tribe. Everything the people say, I shall stay right by it. My brother-in-law has done a great thing. He is going to punish himself in the Sun Dance to bring me back. He won't do it alone, for I am going in too."

All the chiefs had to dance, too, under the conditions stated by the pledger. The dance, which took place near what is now Sheridan, Wyoming, was a memorable one. The spot is still remembered as Where-the-Chiefs-Starved Themselves (Llewellyn and Hoebel 1941:9-12).

It is in the facing up to new crisis situations such as this that the Cheyennes show their real legal genius and their capacity for treating their culture as a working instrument for the realization of social ends.

The introduction of horses, of course, has posed new problems. Theft within the tribe has never been a troublesome matter, for a person receives as a gift anything he asks for, and those who are well off are always giving to their less fortunate fellows. Horses are given away to honor many special occasions. Nonetheless, by 1850 the taking of horses without asking had become a sore point with some owners. The issue was finally brought to a head by Wolf-Lies-Down, whose horse was "borrowed" in his absence. The borrower had left his bow and an arrow in Wolf-Lies-Down's lodge as identification and surety, but after a year he had still not returned the horse. Wolf-Lies-Down put the matter before his military society, the Elk Soldiers. They sent a messenger off to the band where the borrower was staying in order to bring him in. When he did arrive, he was leading the borrowed horse, plus another one. He explained he was sorry he was gone longer than expected and that he was giving Wolf-Lies-Down the second horse as well as the one that belonged to him.

Wolf-Lies-Down said that was fine and from now on he and the other man would be bosom friends (that is, formal "brothers"). The Elks then wound up the whole matter by declaring that it would be that way between the

Elks and the society of the borrower. "Our society and his shall be comrades. Whenever one of us has a present to give, we shall give it to a member of his soldier society."

But there was more. "Now we shall make a new rule. There shall be no more borrowing of horses without asking. If any man takes another's goods without asking, we will go over and get them back for him. More than that, if the taker tries to keep them, we will give him a whipping" (Llewellyn and Hoebel 1941:127-128).

The incident illustrates three points: 1) a neat cleaning up of the immediate sore spot, 2) a formalization of friendship between the individuals who were on the point of becoming potential enemies, with multiple reinforcement of the positive relations by virtue of the entire fraternity taking the same step, and 3) the laying down of a clear legal norm for the future, with the penalty stated for an arrant "borrower." This became a rule for the whole tribe.

A short time later an incorrigible juvenile delinquent, Pawnee, learned to his rue that the rule was to be enforced. He was a notorious horse "borrower" and troublemaker. When he ignored the new law, the Bowstring Soldiers took after him and tracked him down three days out on the trail. They beat him unmercifully, destroyed his clothing and saddle, ruined his gun and everything else he had with him. Alone on the prairie, he was preparing to die, when High Backed Wolf found and rehabilitated him (see above, pp. 37-38).

The Cheyennes are also capable of rejecting proposed new legal norms when they are assessed as potentially dangerous. This happened when Walking Rabbit tried to introduce the Comanche practice of permitting a man to take a woman away from another man by making her a member of a war party. When Walking Rabbit turned up with a stolen wife, the raid was immediately halted and the warriors went into council to consider what should be done about the situation. They flatly rejected the proposition that the wife absconder and his companion should go along with them. Walking Rabbit was sent back home—but again with the cooperative softening of the blow; everyone promised to give Walking Rabbit arrows to send the aggrieved husband. Several promised horses. So it was done. Walking Rabbit's father had already settled the case, when his rash son got back with the girl. When the raiders returned, he proposed that they give the horses and arrows to her kin. This they did in a grand gesture. Her relatives gathered exchange goods. "The war party was called together once more; to them this stuff was given. It was a great thing for the people to talk about. It was the first and last time a woman was sent home on enemy horses the day they came in" (Llewellyn and Hoebel 1941: 13-14).

In this and other new matters of immediate urgency, the fighting men, either as a military society or as an *ad hoc* war party, can "legislate" law, which on the basis of its fundamental soundness finds general acceptance. Such matters need not necessarily go to the council when they do not involve a direct challenge to rules already established under council jurisdiction. Social solidarity and cultural flexibility are attained in a variety of ways.

PART THREE

Subsistence and War

6

Hunting and Gathering

THE HOMELAND of the Cheyennes is the high portion of the Great Plains. It is a vast, grasslands area naturally devoid of trees except along the watercourses and the foothills of the mountains. Its elevation ranges from three to five thousand feet, except in the mountainous portions to the west. Climatically, the entire country is subhumid, the mean annual rainfall varying from only ten to twenty inches a year. A deficiency of water is in fact the distinguishing climatic characteristic. Most of the precipitation falls in the summer, often in the form of stupendous, crashing thunderstorms. The runoff is quick, except where water gathers in buffalo wallows, and the evaporation rate during the hot, dry days is high. The grass is of the short-grass variety. It grows luxuriantly in the late spring and early summer, and at that time the bison gather in immense herds. As summer progresses, the grass dries and becomes sparser; the herds break up into widely scattered foraging units. This is the essential ecological fact controlling the Cheyenne seasonal rhythm of tribal in-gathering and band dispersion.

In addition to facing the searing heat of the summer, the Indian must confront the winds. "The level surface and the absence of trees give air currents free play. On the whole, the wind blows harder and more constantly on the Plains than it does in any other portion of the United States, save on the seashore" (Webb 1931:21). Of the summer winds Ward (1925:405) writes that their characteristics are "their intense heat and their extreme dryness." "Everything" notes Webb, "goes before the furnace blast. . . . A . . . common effect is that these hot winds render people irritable and incite nervousness (we wonder if Cheyenne breakthroughs of personal violence relate to this). The throat and respiratory organs become dry, the lips crack, and the eyes smart and burn." It was under such conditions that Erect Horns went to the Sacred Mountain to learn how to bring forth the game and get rain and verdure from Thunder. Is it any wonder that Cheyenne ceremonies work constantly for world renewal, for the blessed conditions that prevail in the spring and early summer?

In the winter, people must contend with the wind in its opposite extreme in the form of either the "norther" or blizzard. The norther comes with little warning, "often accompanied by a solid sheet of black cloud and clouds of sand, and causes the thermometer to drop with incredible speed from twenty-five to fifty degrees." A personal account of an army wife en route to Ft. Arbuckle in 1867 contains this description:

> The second morning dawned mild and clear, almost summer-like—an ominous quiet soon to be broken by a sound like the roar of the ocean. A gust of wind almost blinded us with dust. The driver exclaimed in terror: "A norther." Hastily we lowered the ambulance curtains, adding buffalo robes as the cold increased to a bitterness that is indescribable. Soon a storm of snow like white sand is whirling all about us. Our mules should have dropped, had not their drivers run at their sides, beating them vigorously. (Eastman 1935:23)

A wet norther is a blizzard, "a mad, rushing combination of wind and snow which neither man nor beast can face." But outface it with their primitive equipage the Cheyennes must—or go under.

The land of the Cheyennes is not a paradise. But, when at its benevolent best, it is a challenging land with the beautiful serenity of vast vistas and the "Big Sky"—a bountiful land of millions of bison and antelope easily taken when the season is right; a land of roots, seeds, and berries for those who know where to find them; a land where a man can get a full, satisfied belly on rich meat balanced with a variety of wild vegetables. But it is still a land where starvation is a spectre never far off, and cold death, thirst, and maddening heat must be ever confronted. It is a land where people must hold together, or perish; where people must "know how," or soon be done in; where the Cheyennes have come to rely not only on technical skill but on mystique and compulsive ritual to bolster their sense of security and give them a faith which will engender courage.

Women's Activities

Men and women cooperate to supply the food, but the division of labor is strict. Women are the vegetable gatherers. The dibble, or digging stick, is their basic tool. It was given by the Great Medicine Spirit and it figures in the ritual paraphernalia of the Sun Dance, for it has its sacred aspects. Cheyenne dibbles are of two types. The short kind has a knob at one end and is pushed under the desired root by pressure against the stomach when the digger is down on both knees. The other kind is long, and used as a crowbar. The sharp ends are fire hardened.

Some eight or ten different wild roots are gathered, including the bulbs of several varieties of lilies. Most conspicuous of the tubers used is the well-known Indian turnip (*Psoralea lanceolata*), also known by the French name, *pomme blanche*. It is dug in the spring when still edible, and is sometimes eaten raw, but more commonly boiled. After cutting it into slices, the Cheyenne women dehydrate it by sun drying for year-long preservation. Dried slices are pulverized and used as a thickening for soup. It is a major source of starch. The "red turnip" (*Psoralea hypogeoe*) is smaller and more tasty, and a great favorite of the Cheyenne palate.

The fruit of the prickly pear cactus (*Optuna polyacantha*) is collected in parfleche bags, worked over with twig brooms to remove the spines, and finally picked clean by the women, who wear deerskin thimbles especially made for the purpose. The fruit is then split, the seeds removed, and the remainder sun dried. The product is added to meat stew and is also used as a soup thickener.

Milkweed buds, collected just before the flower opens, are boiled in soup or stew. The "milk" of the plant is evaporated to make a favorite chewing gum.

Thistle (*Arsium edule*) stalks are peeled and eaten with great pleasure. Cheyennes compare it with the banana as a delicacy.

Many varieties of berries are collected by the women, but most common is the chokecherry (*Prunus melanocarpa*). The whole berry, including the pit, is pulped on stone mortars and made into sun-dried cakes. Mixed with dried, pounded meats, it produces the best pemmican.

Of the wild plants gathered by the women for their family larder, some sixteen varieties are fruits, eight or ten are roots, and a dozen to fifteen are vegetable stalks or buds. Many of them add variety to boiled meat dishes or nourishing quality to soups. The Cheyennes do not bake or fry breads made of plant flour.

Although root digging is a tiresome chore, the girls and women do not treat it as such. They leave the camp in the morning in small work parties without a male guard against enemy marauders. Their spirits are usually gay, for they look on the day's activity as an outing. Far out on the prairie they scatter to their individual tasks, for the actual gathering requires no cooperative effort. When they come together in the late afternoon, they often react to the monotony of their work by gambling their roots against each other in a game of seeing who can throw her digging stick the farthest, or by throwing "dice" of buffalo metacarpals.

If it is *pomme blanche* they have been gathering, they excitedly anticipate the sport with the men that awaits them at the camp. The sport consists of the women making believe they are a war party and the men are their enemies. When not far from the camp, they arrange their roots in a row of piles and take their positions behind them, sitting down. Now one woman rises and signals with her blanket, letting out a great war whoop. In the camp the men start up, and other women rush out to see the fun. The young men grab scrubby old horses and lazy nags. Some snatch women's rawhides from under the pounding stones. Others already have imitation shields of willow twigs. Pounding away on their burlesque war steeds, whooping and hollering like mad, they charge down on the line of root diggers. These await them with ammunition of sticks and chips of dry buffalo manure which they let fly when the men are within range. The men dodge and twist; one who is hit is "wounded" and out of the game. Only one who has had a horse shot under him or has himself been wounded in war may dismount to snatch some roots, if he gets through the barrage unscathed. Others just mill around making a great to-do. When a few roots have at last been captured, the men withdraw to a hill to eat them and joke about their exploits and casualties while the women pick up their burdens and go on into the camp.

Sometimes the men plan a surprise attack during which, after counting a coup, they may make off with some roots. But if the women see them coming, they gather together behind a circle drawn in the ground with a digging stick. This represents a fortified camp, and no man may cross the line unless he has killed an enemy or counted coup within enemy breastworks. He who has done so dismounts after entering the circle, recites his coup, and exercises his privilege of helping himself to as many roots as he wishes to carry away. If there is no man in the party who qualifies for this deed, the women hoot and insult the men who presumed to attack them.

This horseplay reveals several things. In the first place, of course, it provides fun and sport after a day of monotonous work. But its special form is significant. It is clearly a vicarious release of suppressed sex antagonisms: the men attack the women, and the women dare them to do it. Yet the men are at the same time satirically burlesqueing the pretensions of their own superiority to women—save for those few men who are sterling examples of Cheyenne success in warfare. The others are targets of ridicule and hurled refuse from the hands of the uncowed women.

Women also go out in foraging groups to gather wood for their fires. Except for collecting expeditions, however, most of a woman's work when the camp is not moving is in and about the lodge preparing food, dressing hides, sewing and decorating clothing, robes, and lodges. A good woman is cheerful, busy, and skillful. The raising and lowering of tipis is solely the job of women, and they do it with skill and speed. In the more permanent camps they excavate the floor of the tipi four or five inches, leaving a sod bench around the outer part to serve as a foundation for the beds. The bare floor is wetted and packed down. A lodge lining is tied part way up the poles and folded inward over the bench so that no draft blows under the tipi cover on the sleepers. With the help of her children, the lodge mistress gathers bundles of grass to lay on the bench as padding. Mats made of horizontal willow withes which are attached to tripods are raised between the ends of each sleeping place and covered with buffalo robes to form backrests. In well-provided lodges each person therefore has a comfortable chaise longue as well as a private bed. A couple of buffalo robes are enough to keep the sleepers warm and comfortable within the tipi no matter how cold it may be outside. The areas under the backrest tripods form cupboards for the storage of gear and the parfleches of dried food.

The basic household item of the woman is her stone maul—an oval river stone with pecked-out grooves on the short sides around which is fixed a supple willow withe firmly fastened with green rawhide. When dried out, the rawhide shrinks and holds the maul within the handle with the grip of a vise. With the maul she breaks up fuel, drives tipi pegs, and crushes large bones to be cooked in soup. With smaller handstones the housewife crushes her chokecherries and pulverizes her dried meat. The Cheyennes are essentially a Stone Age people.

Every household has its complement of horn spoons. These are made by steaming or boiling the horns of buffalo or mountain sheep until pliable. Tortoise shell and wood are also sometimes used.

Prior to contact with white traders, the Cheyenne women produced a variety of pottery dishes for cooking and serving. By the time covered by this study, however, these had been supplanted by trade goods. Crude wooden bowls and dishes continue to be used. For the carrying and storage of water, "Western" water bags are conveniently fashioned from buffalo pouches, bladders, or pericardia. The general name for water bags, *histaiwitsts* ("heart covering"), suggests the most ancient form.

Each woman has a tanning kit of four tools: a scraper, flesher, drawblade, and softening rope or buffalo scapula (shoulder blade). The scraper is a prepared flat, oval stone held in both hands and used to remove extraneous meat and fat from the inner surface of the hide. Metal scrapers supplied by traders are also used.

The flesher is a more delicate instrument. Shaped like an adze, it is made of an elkhorn handle bent at right angle, with a sharp chipped flint lashed across the short end. It is used to hack down the inner surface of the skin to get it to the right degree of thinness. Its proper use is a high skill, and a good fleshing tool is a cherished family heirloom. Grinnell acquired a flesher that had passed through the hands of five mothers and daughters (all known) and had been in continuous use for about a hundred and fifty years when he received it.

The drawblade is a slightly curved willow stick, into the concave side of which is glued a sharpened bone splinter. With the hide draped over an inclined pole, the woman worker shaves off the hair from the outer side of the skin.

Tanning calls for chemical applications; otherwise, the result is rawhide. Brains, liver, and soapweed provide the essentials of the working compound, which is mixed with grease to provide body. The stuff is well rubbed into both sides of the hide, which is then put to soak overnight. After drying in the sun, it is laboriously softened by being worked back and forth over a rawhide rope or by being pulled through a hole in a buffalo shoulder blade fastened to a tree.

A small lodge requires eleven buffalo cowhides, thinned and tanned. A big lodge takes as many as twenty-one. A woman does all the work on her lodge skins up to the point of the rope- or blade-softening process. For this last step she invites in her friends and relatives—one for each hide—and gives them a big feast. Each one is then given a hide to take home to finish, with a rawhide rope to use for the work. Meanwhile, she has to split and make quantities of thread from the buffalo sinews she has been hoarding. Her next chore is the preparation of another great feast, for the process of cutting and sewing the lodge is an all-day sewing-bee to which all her friends will bring the hides she has parceled out to them. At daybreak she must first seek out a woman known as an expert lodge maker, to whom she supplies paint and a cutting knife. Before the guests arrive, the lodge maker fits the pieces and marks them for cutting. The sewers subsequently arrive for breakfast and work all day long, with a meal in the afternoon and a supper at night—this last after the lodge has been raised and stretched on its foundation. For her pains, the expert lodge maker receives a small present.

A new home is a great thing for all the tribe, and it is so recognized in a ritual of dedication. Except for the women working on it, no one may enter a new lodge until the bravest man available has counted coup on it and has entered, followed by other outstanding warriors. The women have completed a hard and great piece of work, and in this way the men give recognition to their achievement.

All clothing is also made by the women. Unfamiliar with the art of weaving, they tan the necessary skins and loosely tailor the garments for themselves, their men and children. Awls are made of ground-down bones (animal or fish), or thorns. These, with thread and decorative materials, are kept by each woman in a hair-covered leather bag worn at her belt. Dresses are tubular sacks sewn together down the sides and reaching well below the knees. Short sleeves hang down from the shoulders.

Old-type moccasins are made of one piece, with the insole as a flap which is folded under and sewed along the outer edge. A durable rawhide sole is sewed on to this. The result is tough and comfortable footgear. Later types are constructed with a separate upper sewed onto a rawhide sole. They are adorned with porcupine-quill or trade-bead embroidery done in geometric patterns, or with little cone-shaped tinklers of tin, obtained from the white traders.

The essential garment of the male is the breechclout. Without it a man believes he will become unsexed, and so regards it as the magical protector of his virility. It is no more than a soft, square skin worn in front and suspended from a cord around the waist. In ceremony and many dances it is the sole garb. In summer, or on a raid, it may be all that is worn; there may be more, but never less.

In inclement weather, the men add leggings which cover the leg from moccasin top outside to the hip and inside to the crotch. Most of them have long fringes or a flap of deer skin on the outside below the knee; either way, walking makes quite a stir. Men's shirts are fashioned much like women's dresses, except that they reach no more than half-way to the knee and have full sleeves. A fully dressed man looks as though he is wearing trousers with a tunic, although the leggings do not, of course, make real pants. Shirts are highly decorated with quill embroidery, trade beads, or, in special cases, the scalps of enemies sewed along the seams of the sleeves. Buffalo robes round out the cold-weather garb of both sexes.

The quilling of robes is an extra, decorative flourish done as a vowed deed. It is a sacred occupation controlled by the Quillers' Society, mentioned earlier as an honored and exclusive group of select women. A woman or girl not a member of the society has to obtain the help and direction of one member as well as the assistance of the other members. The whole procedure of instruction is highly ritualistic and sacred. The neophyte must provide food and materials. Before the work begins, all the women recite the making of their best pieces—just as a warrior counts coup. An old male crier announces to the whole camp what is being done and publicly invites some poor person to come to see the girl who is going to decorate her first robe. For coming, the visitor receives the gift of a horse, and if he is a man, he rides it around the camp singing a song of praise extolling the giver. Two to four brave warriors are invited to the women's "coup counting," and when the women have told their quilling exploits, the men tell their great war deeds and dedicate the kettle of meat, which is offered to the spirits and divided among the women.

The sewing is done later. If a mistake is made, a warrior who has scalped an enemy must be sent for. He tells his coup and says, "And when I scalped him, this is how I did it," so cutting the misplaced quills loose.

When the Quillers are sewing the lodge decorations, the warriors may "attack" them in a very formal way. They choose a scout who at some time has been the first to spot the enemy, and he goes into the Quillers' lodge to see what they have to eat. He is followed by the bravest of all the men, who counts coup on the pot and is privileged to carry away the food without objection from the women.

Men's Activities

While women gather vegetable foods and make the home and its accoutrements, men bring home the meat, make weapons, wage war, and perform the major part of the necessary rituals.

The Cheyenne men are almost exclusively big-game hunters, even as the postglacial paleo-Indians of the Plains. Bison stand out as their basic staple, with antelope next, then deer, elk, and wild sheep. Smaller game, such as wolves and foxes, are taken occasionally for their furs. Of their domesticated animals, the dog is a favorite delicacy reserved for feasts. "With us, a nice fat, boiled puppy dog is just like turkey at Thanksgiving with you," High Forehead used to say to me. Horsemeat is eaten, but not preferred. As a heritage from their days in the Woodlands, the Cheyennes (unlike most Plains tribes) also take fish.

A superficial paradox governs buffalo hunting. When buffalo are scarce, anyone may hunt when and as he pleases. When they are plentiful, the restrictions of the communal hunt come into force. The reasons for this are clear and simple: while scattered buffalo in small herds cannot be efficiently hunted by large groups, the massive early-summer herds, as already indicated, are best attacked by a closely working, cooperative group.

The communal buffalo hunt is a development stemming from the old-time antelope drive, which was a mystic procedure. Antelopes, as is well known, are the fleetest of animals, adapted to survival by speed of flight. They are at the same time, however, endowed with an odd sense of curiosity. They want to observe any unusual object and will, for instance, move toward a gently moving flag. It is this trait that the Cheyennes seized upon, magically elaborating their exploitation of it. In the nineteenth century, magical antelope surrounds (hunts) have become infrequent, but every now and then some medicine man puts one on. The basic pattern is not confined to the Cheyennes, but is widespread among Indians of the Plains, Great Basin, and Southwest (Underhill 1948:28-34).

The antelope shaman receives his power from Maiyun in a series of dreams. When he feels ready to put on a hunt, the news is passed by word of mouth rather than through a crier. This, and the fact that the shaman also lets it be known that no guns or ordinary weapons are to be used in the hunt, indicates that the pattern was set before the tribe established itself in the Plains, for the crier and gun are both culture traits acquired after the Cheyennes had migrated into the Plains.

As a first step, the shaman raises a small medicine tipi within which he performs an all-night ritual, the details of which are not known. At certain stages, the members of a military society beat on the lodge covering over four of the lodge poles which are mystically endowed. If the hunt is going to be successful, large quantities of antelope hair fall off the lodge covering.

The next morning, the shaman leads the people out toward where his power has told him the antelope will be. The hunters are on their fastest horses, but he is afoot. At the chosen spot, he selects two exemplary virgin girls. They must be good-tempered, or the antelope will be fractious and hard to control. They should also be plump, or the antelope will be skinny and stringy. Each is given a so-called antelope arrow: a wand with a medicine wheel at one end. The shaman has already used these to draw the antelope toward the spot. Each girl begins running outward on diverging, diagonal courses so that their paths begin to describe a wide V. Two young men, supposed to be their suitors, chase after them on the fastest and longest-winded horses available. The hunters on their horses tail out after them in two long lines.

As soon as the hunters are on their way, the remaining women and children form a circle at the foot of the V, with the shaman in the center. As the two leading young men pass the pair of girls, each takes one of the wands the girls have been carrying. They continue on the diverging line for a couple of miles, riding at a fast pace. Soon they are on both sides of an antelope herd, which, instead of running away, turns toward the shaman. The men with the wands then turn in and cross behind the herd, continuing to ride back outside the lines of hunters, who have followed them and entirely surrounded the herd. When the two reach the shaman, they return the wands. Down the V the antelope are driven at a fast pace, pell-mell into the circle of old men, women, and children, who with waving blankets close around them to form a human corral. Using his two wands as directional signals, the shaman makes the antelope rush around and around until they are utterly confused and exhausted. This is the drama that is reenacted in the Crazy Animal Dance. Then the people set upon the befuddled beasts and kill them with clubs. For his pains and skill the shaman receives all the tongues (a choice delicacy) and his choice of two antelope. The two girls and two young men make their choice next. After that, an even distribution is made among all the families.

William Bent, the trader, was with the Southern Cheyenne in 1858 when such a hunt was held under the direction of White Faced Bull. It was so successful that every one of six hundred Cheyenne lodges had an antelope, and Bent's wagon train had all it could use (Grinnell 1923:I, 288).

Other times, antelope are led and driven into a pit or over a bluff in the same way. Occasionally, the V is formed of brush piles behind which people hide until the antelope are between them.

The same technique is also applied to buffalo hunts. On one such occasion some enemy Shoshones turned up just after the hunt was completed. The Cheyennes attacked them in the ordinary battle manner, but afterwards thought it a shame that the Shoshones had not arrived a bit earlier. "We could then have sent those two girls around them and killed them all off just as we had the buffalo" (Hoebel n.d.).

For general purposes, the nonmagical hunt suffices in taking bison. They are not so skittish as the antelope, and the soldier-policed secular hunt is more usable as an everyday affair. In such hunts, when the charge is made, the hunter rides his horse up along the right side of a running beast and sends an arrow down and between its ribs. The horses are trained to follow tight beside the animal so that both the rider's hands are free to use the bow. Strong men sometimes shoot an arrow right through one bison and into another. If a spear is being used, it is driven down with the full force of both arms, between the ribs and into the heart. If a man is not good enough to do this, or conditions are not right, he thrusts for the kidneys, which are easier to reach. This does not bring such a quick kill, but it is a fatal wound with which a buffalo cannot run far. Lances and bows are preferred for large hunts even by those Cheyennes who possess guns, for many more animals can be killed this way; guns are too slow to reload for a man on horseback.

When the hunt is done, the men skin and butcher the take, loading it all on pack horses for the trip back to the camp where it is turned over to the women for cooking or cutting into thin slices which are hung on racks to sun dry. Later, the dried meat is shredded by pounding with the stone mauls and packed away as pemmican.

Deer and elk are taken by individual hunters who stalk them with bow and arrow, or ambush them from hiding places along their trails.

The large gray wolf is taken in pitfalls—deep holes dug wider at the bottom than at the top so that the wolf cannot jump out. A pole with bait at the center is staked across the hole, which is roofed over with split reeds covered with earth and grass. As the wolf moves out on to the mat to seize the bait, the whole covering gives way beneath him. He may then be shot in his prison.

Since foxes are too light to be taken this way, they are caught in dead-falls. In this type of trap two logs are arranged, one on the ground and another supported by a trigger above it. A little willow twig house, open at the deadfall end, is built over the baited trigger. Thus, the fox is forced to put his head under the fall-log if he is to get at the bait. A tug on the lure springs the trap; the log falls on his neck or back, killing or paralyzing him.

Eagles are not eaten but are highly prized for their feathers. They are caught by human hand and strangled. This is a crafty, ticklish undertaking, and one for specialists only—men who have eagle-catching power and knowl-edge of its associated rituals. Eagles have a wingspread up to seven feet and a beak as long as their heads. The trick is done from a pit-blind, which must be painstakingly prepared. The pit can be dug only when there are no eagles in the sky, and the dirt must be scattered a long way off, because eagles are far-sighted and cautious. Before digging the pit, the eagle catcher must sing his sacred eagle songs alone in his lodge all night long. His pit, which is just large enough for him to sit in, is roofed over with long grass through which are left a few spy holes. He deodorizes himself in a sweat bath and greases himself all over with eagle-grease paint. He enters the hole before daybreak, when the eagles cannot see him. Over his head a piece of fresh bait is tied firmly down. When an eagle settles down to tear at the bait, the hunter slowly slips his hands through the grass, grabs its legs and pulls it into the hole. The hunter is then in a 3-by-5 hole with a fighting, clawing eagle that he must strangle with a noose! The reward is considerable prestige and a good return in trade value: a horse for twenty or thirty feathers, for example. Eagle catch-ing must be done in four-day stints (a ritual requirement). At the end, a ceremonial offering and apology are made to the dead eagles, followed by the hunter's taking four sweat baths to neutralize the sacred power worked up for use in the enterprise.

Turtles are taken from ponds and roasted or boiled in the shell for food.

When still in the lake country, the Cheyennes used to seine for fish, setting willow nets into which they drove the fish. Now they construct a fish weir in rivers under the supervision of a medicine man. The weir is a circle made of willow poles driven closely together into the bottom and lashed with rawhide. The weir is left alone at night for the fish to enter, while the medicine man in his lodge tries to draw them into the pen. During the next day, one man works with a long, narrow basket which is placed against an opening made in the downstream side of the weir. As the fish enter his basket, he removes them and tosses them up on the shore for the waiting people.

In summing up, we see that the Cheyennes provision themselves with a fair variety of food that gives a reasonably balanced diet in good times. Their techniques and skills are of a high order; they work together in smoothly cooperative teams for the common weal. Still, they live under feast-or-famine conditions, and famine is never forgotten. So uncertain is their food situation that, except for root- and berry-gathering activities, and the policed, secular buffalo hunts, ritual and supernatural power suffuse their undertakings. They are anything but improvident, and the drying power of the High Plains sun is constantly used to preserve meat and vegetables for leaner times. That the Cheyennes go to such lengths to preserve their food supply, despite the fact that it must all be packed along whenever they move, is indicative of their efforts to maintain their larder.

7

Warfare

THE CHEYENNES fight to hold the place they have won for themselves on the Great Plains. Like all the nomadic tribes, they are relatively recent newcomers to the great buffalo area, and with the Crows, Arapahos, Utes, Comanches, Shoshones, Pawnee, Omahas, Dakotas, and others, jostle for far-ranging hunting grounds. Each tribe maintains peaceful alliances with some tribes and an unrelenting struggle with others. The friendly allies of the Cheyennes are the three Village tribes of the upper Missouri River (Mandan, Hidatsa, and Arikara), the Sioux, the cognate Arapaho, and, as we have seen, since 1840, the Comanche and Kiowa. Their foremost and despised enemy is the Crow tribe on the west, and then the Pawnee to the southeast. The Shoshones and Utes are next. The Sac, Fox, Delaware, and other displaced Woodland tribes, who were driven into the eastern Plains by the whites from 1836 onwards, are all treated as intruding enemies. The Cheyennes do not come up against them often, but they suffered severe defeats in 1853 at the hands of a few Delawares allied to the Pawnee, and again in 1854 at the hands of a hundred Sac and Fox. These eastern tribes are well armed with the best long-range buffalo rifles, which they handle with consummate skill and devastating effect against the Cheyennes, whose tactics are not well suited to the new style of warfare.

From the time of the earliest contacts down to the opening of armed assaults on them by American troops near Fort Laramie, Wyoming, in 1854, the Cheyennes were entirely friendly with the Americans. The southern bands entered into intimate and friendly relation with the Bent family of traders, who opened their famous trading post on the Arkansas in 1837. Once the United States Army took up arms against the Cheyennes, however (see Introduction, p. 2), the wars with the United States have been unceasing. They ended with the final shattering of the Cheyenne power to resist in 1878.

Living as they do in an atmosphere of chronic warfare, the Cheyennes, like other Plains tribes, emphasize military virtue. There are at least

a hundred different situations in the ritual life of the people that invite ceremonial coup counting by an outstanding warrior. Public glory is the ever-
present reward of the man who fights bravely and well. The fighting patterns
of the Cheyennes are embellished with virtuosities that go far beyond the
needs of victory. Display in bravery tends to become an end in itself. Prestige
drives override the more limited military requirements for defeat of the enemy.
The show-off tends to supersede the mere soldier. War has been transformed
into a great game in which scoring against the enemy often takes precedence
over killing him.

The scoring is in the counting of coup—touching or striking an enemy
with hand or weapons. Coups counted within an enemy encampment rank
highest of all. By extension, any heroic deed in battle counts as a coup: saving
a wounded comrade, being first to locate the enemy, having a horse shot out
from under one, or charging a body of enemies alone while the rest of the
Cheyennes watch to see the result. A man's rank as a warrior depends on two
factors: his total "score" in coups and his ability to lead successful raids in
which Cheyenne losses are low. Actual killing and scalping get their credit, too,
but they do not rate as highly as the show-off deeds. Closely allied to war is
horse stealing, because any raid for horses can provoke a battle.

Cheyenne war parties are of three kinds: private, fraternity, and tribal.
Of these, the first is by far the most common. Any properly qualified Cheyenne
can assemble a war party; he need only engage the interest of a few friends.
Since most men are caught up in the drive for military prestige, this is not
hard to do—especially among the young men who still have their reputations
to make. The older men who have secured their reputations and have responsi-
bilities as peace chiefs or medicine men are not ordinarily so eager for the warpath as are the youngsters. The war leaders are those who have proven their
skill on the warpath but who are not yet old enough or lack the personal
attributes to be tribal chiefs or medicine men. The war chiefs are the officers of
the military societies, but one does not have to have achieved that degree of
eminence to lead a private war party. One needs only to be good.

Cheyenne custom does not require a vision endorsement of an inclina-
tion to lead a war party, as is true of some tribes. Nonetheless, as is the case
with every important activity among the Cheyennes, a beginner must be instructed by a medicine man and must secure a ritualized right to undertake the
mission. Cheyenne boys normally join their first war party when only fourteen
or fifteen years of age. They are solicitously watched over by the older men
and are not expected actively to engage in fighting, but they get their taste of
danger and accumulate experience early. By twenty they are seasoned warriors. By thirty, or earlier, they are ready to lead their own raids, if they have
the necessary leadership qualities.

When the time comes, an aspiring war leader invites an experienced
older man to help him. He offers his pipe and explains his wish. Most commonly he is told to make an offering to the Sacred Arrows, or perhaps to hang
himself from a pole in the hills. If it is to be an offering to the Arrows, he fills

his pipe, dons a buffalo robe hair side out, and walks to the lodge of the Arrow Keeper, wailing as he goes, so that everyone will know what he is about. At the door of the lodge, he stands and wails until the Arrow Keeper invites him in. The Keeper smokes the suppliant's pipe, thereby acknowledging his readiness to help him. The suppliant ritually consecrates the offering, which, under the Keeper's direction, is then tied to the Arrow Bundle. During the course of this act, the young man prays to the Arrows, asking for success in his new venture.

Now he is ready to lead war parties. He calls together some friends and other men who he thinks will make good and willing companions. First, he feeds them. Then he tells them what is in his mind. He passes his pipe, and all who have decided to accept his leadership smoke. The others pass it by. After a while, those who have pledged themselves go together to the tipi of a ceremonial priest or some good medicine man for ritual preparation. They take him a filled pipe, telling him they wish to go to war. If he approves the plan, he smokes and sings a sacred war song. He may tell them which way to go and where they may expect to find their enemies. They now have "official" sanction for their venture.

Still later, they may bring some war article—a shield, bonnet, or weapon —to be consecrated in a sweat lodge as a talisman of good luck and protection. Various members of the party may cut strips of skin from their arms to leave as sacrifices to the spiritual powers.

Now they get ready their gear. The night before their departure, painted and stripped for action, they parade around the camp, singing wolf songs—for the wolf is associated with war—and receiving little presents from the people who wish them well.

A war party of this type is breaking itself off from the society for a while. Consequently, it does not leave as a body, nor is there any display at the time of the departure. The leader starts out alone early the next day. The members have an appointed rendezvous not far from the first night's camping place. From this spot, they all proceed together in single file, with the leader in front carrying his pipe. At the camp site they smoke, pray, and sing holy war songs. At last, when all the others are asleep, the leader chants a prayer for help, courage, and wisdom.

So they proceed until they reach the danger ground. Once there, they move by cautious stages, with two scouts well in advance. These move under cover to an elevation where they can scrutinize the country ahead. They not only look for human beings, camps, and smoke, but they study the actions of birds and animals for the characteristic signs and actions they show when people are near. If all is clear, the scouts signal their followers to advance, while they move on to the next point of observation.

Small, private raiding parties of this kind are out either to take horses or to get a scalp in revenge for the death of a friend or relative. If the first object is their goal, they seek to avoid a fight and will sneak into the enemy camp at night to drive off its herd under the cover of darkness. If it is scalps they are after, they prefer to come upon lone travelers, small isolated family camps, or parties of hunters. If they find a camp, and they are not discovered, they take time to prepare their war medicines and paint themselves. Otherwise, they attack as the opportunity offers.

Big war parties are almost always revenge expeditions. When a Cheyenne raiding party has been wiped out or a considerable number of casualties have been suffered by an attack on a Cheyenne camp, someone is almost sure to get a hundred or more warriors together for a punitive expedition. He takes his pipe from camp to camp, gathering recruits. Or he may go to several military societies to enlist their members. Such an outfit is still essentially a private war party, because it is the affair of the man who initiates it.

Because the membership of the military societies is (with the exception of the Dog Soldiers) scattered through all the bands, war parties are rarely constituted of members from one fraternity only. It may be also that the disastrous annihilation of the Bowstring Soldiers by the Kiowas in 1837 discouraged what might have been a more prevalent practice in earlier times. In the Cheyenne's mind, that event proves the power of the Sacred Arrows and the disastrous effects of disrespect for them. The Cheyennes and Arapahoes were camped together near Bents' Fort while the Arapahoes were holding a Sun Dance. No Cheyenne war parties had been out for some time, because there had been a killing in the tribe. An Arrow Renewal had been pledged, but Grey Thunder, the Arrow Keeper, was postponing the rite until the Arapaho ceremony was finished. Restless Cheyenne warriors were not interested in the Arapaho doings; they wanted their Arrows renewed so that they could get off to war. The Bowstrings were especially eager. At last the Bowstrings arrogantly demanded that the Arrows be renewed, and when Grey Thunder refused, they actually beat him. He then consented, but prophesied disaster for them. The war party of forty-two Bowstrings, after a long and exhausting trip on foot during which they used up most of their arrows hunting game, finally found a big Kiowa camp. Their scouts were seen before they were ready to attack, and the Kiowas greatly outnumbered them. As a result, the Cheyennes were cut off and forced to make a stand. With few arrows they could not long defend themselves, and so died to a man.

This is the kind of loss that provokes the entire tribe to go on the war path in revenge. In this particular case, Porcupine Bear, head chief of the Dog Soldiers, undertook to organize the war party. He set out to devote the winter to the task, carrying his pipe and a barrel of whiskey obtained from some trader. The whiskey was his undoing, for at one camp there was a drunken brawl and Porcupine Bear killed a man. He was exiled, and his close kin went with him. After the Renewal of the Arrows in the summer of 1838, Little Wolf, chief of the Bowstrings (later the Sweet Medicine Chief of the entire tribe), took up the task. So much time was required to call in the northern bands that by the time they were assembled, winter was again at hand. The camp circle was at last complete, and a large arbor for the military societies was placed in its center. Here all the fraternities convened to receive the relatives of the forty-two dead men, who came to them with horses and presents. Their arms streaming blood from their mourning gashes, the women passed their reeking hands over the soldiers, asking them to take pity on them. The soldiers agreed. But then came a big snow, and the tribe had to break up, for there was not feed enough for all the horses. When spring came, they reassembled.

On a tribal war move, the Arrow and Buffalo Hat Bundles play an important part. They are carried on the backs of their Keepers' wives, and four stops must be made for their ritual use. Before the big attack, after the enemy has been sighted, there is a massive ritual preparation of the Arrows culminating in the pointing of the two man Arrows at the enemy, who, it will be remembered, are supposed to be blinded by their brightness and confused by their power. The Arrows are then lashed to the lance of a great warrior and carried by him into the thick of the battle. The Buffalo Hat is worn by another warrior—and so success is assured. A tribal attack is a big event (it has happened only six times in all Cheyenne history: against the Shoshones in 1817, the Crows in 1820, Pawnees in 1830, Kiowas and Comanches in 1838, and Pawnees in 1853) and it calls for the risk of their biggest medicines. The Kiowa-Comanche assault was ill fated, as had been the War of 1830 against the Pawnees, because the battle started before the Arrow preparations were completed. In this instance, Porcupine Bear and his followers were tagging along behind the main body of Cheyennes and their Sioux and Arapaho collaborators, who were along for the fun. On the day of the battle, Porcupine Bear and his six male cohorts lured thirty-seven Kiowa buffalo hunters into an ambush so successfully executed that the seven outlaw Cheyennes killed every man in the Kiowa group. They received no coups for their great achievement because they were outlaws—and perhaps because they ruined the power of the Arrows. The main attack, while it inflicted considerable damage on the enemy ranks, resulted in the death of an unusually large number of Cheyenne chiefs and notables. Grey Thunder, smarting from his treatment by the Bowstrings the year before, let himself be killed at the outset of the fight. He had said, "I will now give the people a chance to get a smarter man to guide them. They have been calling me a fool" (Grinnell 1915:42-59; for an account of the organization of the tribal move against the Crows, see Llewellyn and Hoebel 1941:3-6). Two years later the Cheyennes, Kiowas, and Comanches decided they had had enough of massive killing and the Peace of 1840 was effected.

It is often said that Indians fight as a howling, unorganized mob, each man for himself. This is not true in general, and certainly not true for the Cheyennes in particular. The tactics of attack and battle are carefully planned by the leaders, and when faithfully carried out often result in a successful clash. The Cheyennes do not ordinarily aim for total victory, but for glory, revenge, and the inflicting of some humiliation and punishment on the enemy. Set battles are therefore avoided, and the tactics are those of stealth, surprise, and maneuver. If the enemy is alerted and well prepared behind earthworks or in a camp with the tipis set edge to edge as a defensive fortification, the

Cheyennes will not ordinarily come to close grips with them. Since the aims of their war do not call for "taking" an enemy position, they withdraw to try again another time. The tribal numbers are small and they cannot stand too many battle losses. In the great attack on the Crows in 1820, Two Twists, who had organized the affair, had vowed to drive the Crows out of their breast-works and die doing it. While all the Cheyennes watched, he charged alone straight into the Crow camp, armed only with a sabre. He fought like a demon and could not be brought down (largely because it happened that most of the Crow fighters were away on their own warpath). Fired by his example, the other Cheyennes charged and broke through, killing or capturing everyone in the camp.

Many unforeseen events may upset the plans of the Cheyenne war lead-ers, but the most plaguing difficulty is the propensity of the scouts to attack enemy stragglers in an effort to get a coup. Too often the result is that the enemy is alerted and the planned strategy upset. The leader of a private war party can do nothing about this. On the tribal moves, however, the enterprise is policed; scouts who slip in such a way are beaten just as though they had broken the rules of the communal hunt.

Cheyenne feats of bravery are legendary. Yet they are by no means supermen. They live from day to day knowing that every hunt exposes them to unannounced attack; every night when they lie down to rest they know that dawn will bring the possibility of an enemy attack on their herds or on their camp. For them, there is no such thing as security—ever. There are no inter-ludes of peace to give surcease from war. When the lurking threat of enemy attacks is not working on them, there is always the knowledge that to qualify as men at all they must themselves go seek out the enemy. Fear haunts them, even though they rarely let it break through to the surface. The evidence is everywhere—the masochistic tortures of hanging from the pole to bring good luck in war, the offering up of cut strips from the arms before starting on the warpath, the faith in the blinding powers of the Arrows, the elaborate rules of smoking and painting in connection with the warpath, the reliance on amu-lets and tabus to give immunity in battle, the great store set by medicine shields. Grinnell thinks the shield is perhaps the most important part of the equipment of the Cheyenne warrior:

> Most shields were believed to possess strong spiritual power. It might exercise in behalf of him who carried it not only the general protective influence due to its sacred character, but it might also endue him with those qualities attributed to the heavenly bodies, birds, mammals, and other living creatures whose images were painted on it, or portions of which were tied to it. . . . A shield adorned with the feathers of the eagle was believed to give its owner the swiftness and courage of that bird. If the feathers of the owl were tied on it, the man perhaps shared the owl's power to see in the dark, and to move silently and unnoticed. The figure of a bear painted on the shield, or its claws attached, gave him the bear's toughness; and so many of the qualities which belonged to the animals which the Cheyennes regarded as possessing superhuman powers. (Grinnell 1923:I, 187-188)

Cheyenne shields are of two major classes: the sacred shields, just described, and ordinary, undecorated shields which are without power. The first class also subdivides into traditional shields belonging to a warrior society or kindred. The group shields of a particular organization are all similar. The second subcategory consists of dream shields, the pattern and power of which have been revealed to their owners in visions.

The technical construction of all shields is alike. The hide of a buffalo bull is thickened and toughened by steaming. The finished shield is round and only eighteen inches or so in diameter. If it is a power shield, it requires an antelope-hide cover on which the medicine symbols are painted.

No man may decorate a shield for the first time without the aid and direction of an established shield maker, who has himself acquired the right by previous instruction. The actual shield painting requires ritual help and dedication by a number of other brave fighters. They decorate themselves with bird feathers and shut themselves in the shield maker's lodge with him. The process begins with ceremonial smoking and the singing of a sacred song. The shield owner then paints a part of his design, after which the pipe is refilled and everyone smokes around the circle. Four songs are sung, and the painting is resumed. This cycle is repeated again and again, until the painting is finished. At last, the cover is fitted to the shield, and the feathers and other objects are added. When this has been done, everyone rubs himself all over with white clay in a first step toward removing the supernatural atmosphere so that he may again enter into ordinary affairs. The female relatives of the owner pass in food, and they eat.

The shield is now put near the door of the lodge where it may be touched by a multitude of men, women, and children, who are called in to get a share of its protective effect. The ceremony is completed with a final purification in which the shield is placed on top of a sweat lodge, raised a few yards in front of the tipi, and all the participants in the painting take a sweat bath while singing sacred shield songs.

A shield thereafter receives very special treatment. It is not kept in its owner's lodge, but rests on a tripod or pole outside of it. Each shield has its special requirements of preparation for use. The owner of one shield told a borrower that it had to be purified in juniper smoke before using. In addition,

When you put the cover on, the deerskin strings which hold the bear-claws must be loosened, so that they may lie down; but when you take the cover off, and go into a fight, the strings must be tightened, so that the claws will stand out stiff, and be directed toward the enemy. When purifying the shield you must pass it over the smoke in the four directions and last hold it over the smoke, and then raise it toward the sky and shake it. Then you must move it four times toward the right front of your body, and hang it over your body on the right side. In riding forward toward the enemy, you must keep on the right-hand side of your party, and quite away from them. Some shields may be supported on a single pole, but this must be on a tripod. In the morning it must be hung out facing the sun. (Grinnell 1923:I, 194)

This is but one reason why the Cheyennes need time to prepare their powers before going into battle. Failure to fulfill any one requirement will almost certainly cause a man to be wounded or killed. The misuse of a shield requires a long, and sometimes strong, ceremony of atonement and purification. The group shields of the Hair Rope band impose an injunction against eating the heart of any animal, or any meat that has been boiled in a stew along with heart. If the prohibition is violated, the shield user must eat the heart of an enemy—something the Cheyenne finds difficult and disagreeable to do.

War bonnets have essentially the same quality as shields; they are not just something that is made and worn. The great warrior, Roman Nose, owed something of his success to his war bonnet, which gave him immunity to bullets. With this bonnet went the tabu that he could eat no food taken from the pot with a pointed, iron utensil. The psychological association is clear. As the pointed implement pierces the food, so will a pointed metal bullet pierce the flesh. Just before the big fight with Colonel Forsythe's command at Beecher Island in 1868, Roman Nose had been entertained in the Sioux camp. Ignorant of his guest's tabus, his host served him fried bread taken from the pan with a fork. A Dog Soldier noticed it and told Roman Nose. The fight with the Americans began before Roman Nose was able to go through his long purificatory rite, so, like Achilles, he stayed in his tent while the battle dragged on. Finally, he gave in to the pleas that he come forth to lead his men. He put on his war bonnet, and while riding up to the battlefield, he was shot and mortally wounded. He did not even get into the fight (Grinnell 1915:275-277).

War ponies must also be supernaturally fortified, if they are to be of the best quality. A man who is well equipped with a string of horses rarely rides his favorite battle steed except in a fight. When off on a mounted raid, he rides an ordinary horse and leads his fighting pony. To insure the quality of such a horse, he selects a yearling that has good prospects and takes it with his pipe to a shaman who has horse medicine. He tells the medicine man he has vowed not to ride the horse for several months, and asks to have it dedicated. After smoking, the medicine man tells him something like this:

> Every night, lead him in and groom him well. Then just turn him loose. He'll run right back to the herd. When he runs back, you get on a hill and watch him. If he lies down, rolls around, and gets up and shakes himself, he is showing that he knows you have promised him something. If you really mean what you have promised here, go out and kill a buck antelope. Take one prong of the horns. We will polish it down and bore a hole in it. Then I will get *mutstintants* to fill the horn with. Fasten two buckskin thongs to the horn and tie it snugly about your pony's neck. If it gets tight, loosen it; it shows that your pony is fattening. Do not ride him at all until the time is up. Then bring him to me. (Hoebel n.d.)

When the promised time has elapsed, the owner leads the horse to the medicine man. He talks to the pony, saying, "Now your months are up. He is going to ride you. Wherever he goes, he'll take you with him." To dedicate a horse and then break the promise not to ride it before its time will kill the horse and bring its owner bad luck.

This performance reveals clearly the Cheyenne feeling about male sexuality—that it is something to be husbanded and kept in reserve as a source of strength for the great crises of war. *Mutstintants* is a root of the species *Cogswellia,* the Cheyenne name of which refers to *motse,* the term for a male, or breeder, among large animals; in other words, the Cheyennes associate this root with animal virility and strength. The phallic symbolism of the antelope horn and the powdered root within it is anything but obscure.

The Scalp Dance that follows a successful raid by a large war party shows in turn how the Cheyennes associate victory with sex properly controlled. Scalping among American Indians is the equivalent of head hunting in other parts of the world. The purpose of both head taking and scalping is to add the supernatural power and life force to that of the victor.

The Cheyenne Scalp Dance is run by the tribal berdaches, or transvestites, as masters of ceremony. The transvestites are male homosexuals who wear women's clothes and often serve as second wives in a married man's household. The Cheyennes call them *hemaneh,* Halfman-halfwoman. There are only five of these in the tribe, all members of the same kindred, the Bare Legs family. They are all doctors and highly respected. War parties like to have Halfmen-halfwomen along, not only for their medical skill, but because they are socially graceful and entertaining. Young people like them because they possess the most powerful of all love medicines. A suitor who is able to get their help is fortunate indeed, for no girl can resist the power of their potions. They are especially sought out as intermediaries to lead the gift-laden horses to a girl's household when a marriage proposal is being made. These people, through sexual sublimation—with their self-abstinence and denial of their natural-born sex—seem to achieve great power. Although we have no *direct* evidence for it, it appears probable that their presence on war parties is desired mainly because of their high "psychological" potential of stored-up virility—which is just what the Cheyennes feel is necessary for successful fighting.

A successful war party is one which has taken enemy scalps without the loss of a single Cheyenne, unless the dead Cheyenne had counted coup before being killed. If but one Cheyenne is killed without first counting coup, any scalps the others have taken are thrown away. If, however, the Cheyennes have been successful in the fighting, with scalps and no losses, the scalps are brought back for a Scalp Dance. The fact that on the return from the battle all the scalps are placed in the custody of the Halfmen-halfwomen indicates that the warriors feel their success is due to the presence of these personages. The fact that the victory dance is a courting dance wholly directed by the Halfmen-halfwomen emphasizes the relation of war to virility. The affirmation of power over their enemies is the assertion of Cheyenne virility. It is for this that virility must be husbanded and receives its apotheosis in the victory celebration of the Dance of the Scalps.

The Scalp Dance is no wild, frenzied affair (as most whites imagine it to be); rather, it is a sociable courtship dance, made up of several parts. It takes place about a huge bonfire prepared by the transvestites, and called a "skunk." The singers for the dance are middle-aged men, all married. They stand in a line to the west of the skunk, facing east. The young men line up north of the fire, the young girls across from them, on the south. Old men and women fill in the eastern side of the square. Only the Halfmen-halfwomen, with their scalps on scalp poles in their hands, are allowed within the square.

The first dance is the Sweetheart's Dance. The young men file around the drummers and line up behind the girls. Each takes the arm of a girl partner, and they dance side by side. The old men and women dance by themselves in their places, some of the women dancing with scalps taken in previous raids. The Halfmen-halfwomen dance before the drummers, waving the newly won scalps. The old men and women clown and burlesque their dancing, trying to make the watchers laugh.

The Courtship, or Sweetheart Dance, is followed by a Matchmaking Dance. In this dance, the old people only look on. The Halfmen-halfwomen split up and go down the lines of boys and girls, asking them who their favorite partners might be. They compare notes in the center, while the dancers wait expectantly. Now they go to the boys, and one by one lead them by their robes to stand next to the girls who are designated for them. Girls and boys are alternated in the line. When every girl has a partner, the dancing begins. Here the girls dance alone, with their backs to the boys. They first dance forward, to the center of the square, and then backward, without turning, to their places beside the boys. There is nothing intimate about this, nothing remotely sensual; it is as formal as the Cheyenne marriage bid. The boys may attain proximity to the girls, but the girls dance away from them, back and away, back and away. Courting is an uncertain business.

A Round Dance is next. On command of the transvestites, the two lines of boys and girls dance up to each other, and then away, but still facing each other. The girls are not so coy or quite so elusive. This movement goes on for some time, when the "callers" cry out, "Choose your partners." Each girl and boy moves across the square to the one for whom he or she had been chosen in the Match-making Dance. Now they all form a circle with their arms about each others' waists. With short, side-stepping movements they dance clockwise, with the old folks in the middle, whooping and hollering, and waving their scalps. The transvestites keep back the children, who crowd too close to watch, by waving their scalps at them from outside the circle.

After a while, the pattern is changed. The Halfmen-halfwomen call, "Girls to the middle and the men to close up." The boys have "captured" their mates. They dance in a ring around the girls while every once in a while the bolder ones among them slip into the middle and hug their girls, arms around their necks. When there has been enough of this, they break up, and all parties go back to form the beginning square.

Now follows what the Cheyennes call the Slippery Dance. It, too, is replete with symbolic significance. Mating is a reciprocal affair. In the previous dance, the boys showed they had the girls. Now the girls show they have got their men. Dancing in pairs, the girls move up to the line of boys, each getting a good hold on the robe of her partner and leading him out to the center. As the girls dance, the young men tag meekly along in tow. They stay that way until their sisters come out to "set them free" by making a present of a bracelet or ring to the girls who have their brothers. Thus, female siblings assert their claim on their brothers, but at a price paid to his new "wife." Wives' rights to a man's loyalty take precedence over his sister's, but a sister is not cut off entirely by his marriage.

The final dance, signifying the culmination of courtship and mating, is the Galloping Buffalo Bull Dance. The women take time out to tie their long skirts up around their legs; then the leaders tell everyone to sit down in his place. The drumming and singing begin. Three or four women get up and go over to where the young men are sitting. They bend over, turn around, and dance with their backs to the men, dancing like buffalo. Soon the men—as many as there are women dancing—spring up, and stooping over like buffalo bulls go prancing along behind the women. More and more women lead on the men, until all the dancers are bounding in a long row like a worked-up herd of buffalo. At last, the Halfmen-halfwomen call, "Go 'round in a circle." Everybody stands up and goes into the Round Dance, and drummers and singers, mating couples and old people, are reunited in one, closed, happy, collective unity. They all sing together as they dance and morning dawns.

PART FOUR

World View and
the Cheyenne Personality

8

World View and Religion

T HE MAJOR ORIENTATIONS of the Cheyenne world view and some of its manifestations in religious and ritual behavior have already revealed themselves in earlier chapters. In this chapter and the following, we shall more explicitly examine the underlying assumptions formulated by the Cheyennes as to the nature of the universe and man.

Gregory Bateson has rightly written, "The human individual is endlessly simplifying and generalizing his own view of his environment; *he constantly imposes on this environment his own constructions and meanings;* these constructions and meanings are characteristic of one culture as opposed to another" (quoted in Kluckhohn 1949:356, italics ours). Or, as Kluckhohn has phrased it,

> Each different way of life makes its own assumptions about the ends and purposes of human existence, about ways by which knowledge may be obtained, about the organization of the pigeonholes in which each sense datum is filed, about what human beings have a right to expect from each other and the gods, about what constitutes fulfillment or frustration. Some of these assumptions are made explicit in the lore of the folk; others are tacit premises which the observer must infer by finding consistent trends in word and deed. (Kluckhohn 1949:359)

Such assumptions and premises are the basic postulates underlying each culture: postulates which define the nature of things are classed as existential postulates; those which qualitatively fix the desirability or undesirability of things or acts are normative postulates. Human perception and human evaluation are colored and shaped by the underlying cultural postulates which are the foundation of knowledge and belief. Man sees all things through a culturally tinted lens.

In examining the major Cheyenne assumptions and values, we find first a rather striking combination of vitalistic and mechanistic attitudes toward the universe. The cosmology of the Cheyennes is in terms of the "world" rather than the "universe." The sun and stars figure prominently in their concerns (the moon less so), but more as outer extensions of a system of which the earth is the largest element. There is no hint of a boundless universe of vast astral systems, such as is characteristic of modern scientific cosmology.

The Cheyenne world is very much a dynamic, operative system of inter-related parts. Each one, however, is governed by a spirit being: the Spirit Who Rules the Universe, the Spirit Who Rules the Summer, the Spirit Who Gives Good Health, the Big Holy People Who Know Everything. The major forces are, therefore, animistic. This is the basic vitalistic fact of Cheyenne thinking. It is assumed that these and most lesser spirit beings are beneficent; they want things to be pleasant and satisfying. They are generous in their blessings upon mankind. They are not niggardly and withholding by nature. They are not vindictive, punishing, cruel, or fearsome; neither Cheyenne religion nor world view rests on fear of the "Gods." Nor are they creators. Cheyenne mythology gives scant attention to questions of how the world was made. It *is*. The great attributes of the spirits lie, rather, in their *knowledge*. They know how to make the universe run properly and how to get the most out of it. Their role, therefore, is that of instructor of men. They are the great teachers. This concept expresses the Cheyenne view that the universe is essentially a mechanical system which is good in essence, but which must be properly understood and used to keep it producing what man needs and wants. The great spirits understand the nature of its working; they know the techniques that help it to produce. This knowledge they willingly share with mankind, if mankind seeks and listens respectfully. Thus the culture-hero myths centering on Sweet Medicine and Erect Horns are accounts of pilgrimages to the fountainheads of knowledge, the homes of the Holy Ones in the Sacred Mountain. The point is important: the greatness of the major spirits is not in their ability supernatur-ally to create and manage things, but in their wisdom about the working of things.

So it is that the great rituals were taught to the legendary knowledge seekers, who in turn carefully taught them to their fellow Cheyennes. So it is that he who has learned a ritual becomes a teacher in the later performances of that ritual. The Pledger of an Arrow Renewal or a Sun Dance, the Quiller of a first robe, is taught step by step the performance of the rite. Even the leader of a first war party must learn the preliminary rites from a knowledg-able priest. Every Cheyenne ritual of consequence has at least a Teacher and a Novice in its personnel.

In content, Cheyenne rituals are compulsive actions rather than verbal petitions. As stated by the Reverend Rudolph Petter, a Mennonite missionary with an intimate knowledge of the Cheyennes based upon many years of asso-ciation with them, "In religious ceremonies, the rites, not the words, are of most importance" (Petter 1907:477). The acts are effective forces in them-selves; they work directly upon the mechanical system of the universe. As an analogy, we might say that the Cheyenne ceremonies are "tune-up jobs," or—in the case of the Arrow Renewal Rites—major overhauls of a machine that has got out of adjustment or suffered a major breakdown in one of its parts.

There is no evidence that the Cheyennes have any explicit energy theory, but it is clearly evident that they have some sort of an implicit energy concept. The total energy charge of any object, and of the world itself, is thought of as limited. As it is expended through activity, it is dissipated and diminished. Thus plants wither, animals become scarce, the earth runs down. Renewal through regeneration is necessary, if men are to survive. The ceremonies produce a recharge and readjustment of the parts so that the whole operates at its full potential once more.

This notion is clearly revealed in the Cheyenne attitude toward sex. Sexual energy is a limited quotient which must be spent sparingly. Therefore, the man of strong character and good family vows at the birth of his first child (especially if it is a boy) not to have another child for either seven or fourteen years. All of the father's growth powers are then concentrated on the development of this one child rather than being dissipated among several. It is necessary to understand that more than the semen of conception goes into growing a child; there is a continuing transfer of the father's "energy" from parent to offspring. The dedication of a child by this means is quite similar to the development of the war pony (described in the last chapter) through abstention and ritual performance. During the long period of seven or fourteen years the father must practice absolute celibacy, unless he has more than one wife. The mother of the dedicated child is without question celibate throughout the period, unless her husband pledges an Arrow Renewal or Sun Dance, when for that specific occasion she may engage in sexual union with the instructing priest. Adultery is so rare among the Cheyennes that it hardly provides an available, if irregular, outlet for sexual desires. Should a parent break the vow of dedication, it is believed it will kill the child. Not many Cheyenne men feel strong enough to submit themselves to the test of self-control demanded for the sake of a child in this act of renunciation, but for those who do, there is the highest of social esteem. My own close friend, High Forehead, was one who did it. There was, in fact, a fifteen-year gap between the birth of his first and second child. His eldest son, when I knew him, was a most superior individual, physically and mentally. High Forehead was quietly proud of the part he felt he played in making him so. "I slept with my wife all that time," he told me, "but I never had sexual relations with her." In his old age, he was one of the most honored men among the Cheyennes.

The Cheyenne in no sense believes that he can control nature. Although his environment is hard and life is precarious, he sees it as a good environment. It is one, however, with which he must keep himself in close tune through careful and tight self-control. Sweet Medicine and Erect Horns warned the ancients of the decline of the Cheyennes which would take place if they failed to act as they were instructed. The prescribed motions and symbolic acts of the numerous ceremonies must be exactly performed as set in tradition, if they are to produce the desired results in earth regeneration, good health, good hunts, and victory. "If the sacred acts were not performed correctly and in proper order . . . it was the obligation of the members of the ceremony to intervene. If all of the officiants erred, a strong wind would arise to warn them of a breach" (Anderson 1956:98). Here, then, is a behavioral response to the Cheyenne view of the mechanics of their systematic universe. Human aspirations are realizable not so much through the appeasement of whimsical spirit beings and gods as through action that fits the conditions of environmental organization and functioning. Man must fit his behavior to the requirements of those conditions, which are impersonal, rather than seek an emotional dependence upon individual creatures. In this respect, the Cheyenne view of the universe has much in common with that of the Pueblo Indians, except that Puebloans feel much more strongly that individual misbehavior throws the whole universe out of balance. The Cheyennes apply this latter notion only to intratribal killings.

The Cheyenne medicine man is consequently more of a priest than he is a shaman. The main road to supernatural power is through acquisition of ritual knowledge learned from one who is already a priest. Such knowledge is technical knowledge, effective when put to use as a "manual of procedures."

Nonetheless, a component of vitalistic animism is also present in the Cheyenne world view. Individual Cheyennes do seek supernatural power on the vision quest; they do share the Guardian Spirit Complex so characteristic of many other North American tribes. A man who wants personal power for healing or immunity in battle may fast in a lonely place and beg the spirits for indulgence and aid. If favored by a spirit, he receives a blessing along with instructions as to how to prepare specific amulets and how to paint himself and what to sing to evoke the power. He is further given the tabus that qualify its use and protection. Visions also come unsought in time of distress, as in the case of the girl who founded the tribal council, or the case of Owl Friend, who founded a new Bowstring Soldier Society on the basis of a dream that came upon him as he lay exhausted in the snow when lost in a blizzard. Guardian spirits are called *maiyunahu'ta,* Spirit Who Told Me in Sleep. The individual Cheyenne who wishes to become in tune with the animistic powers of the universe, however, does it not so much through fasting and vision seeking as through the sacrificial offering. The pledging of a ceremony is an offering in exchange for help. Gifts are given to the Medicine Arrows and Sun Dance Lodge. Skin is cut from the arms, and men hang from the pole or drag buffalo skulls.

> One offered to the *maiyu*ⁿ . . . food, tobacco, a blanket or some calico, or a white bison hide, an arrow or a root digger, an enemy scalp, a finger joint, a strip or [*sic*] skin or a bit of flesh, or a ritual or ceremony. . . . In a narrow sense it was giving; *in a wider sense, simply doing, that which was valued by the supernaturals.* The gifts or acts were traditional and standard, which is to say, culturally prescribed; *the goal or response was a concrete return*—health for oneself or kin, a wealth of horses, many coups on a raid, success in the hunt, or a shaman's powers. (Anderson 1956:102; italics ours)

The important point is that even the Cheyenne spirit beings respond to acts in a quite mechanical way.

The Cheyenne world view is action oriented. The Cheyennes are not given to philosophical speculation; they do not draw fine elaborations of the metaphysical characteristics of spirits or deities; they do not seek mystic withdrawal from life in the Oriental manner. Whether the fact that their language is built upon verbs has any causal tie with this striking feature of their culture, we cannot say—but the possibility ought not be overlooked.

The Cheyennes have a small core of ancient beliefs about spirits other than the four groups of the spirits of the major directions. There is the all-knowing high god, *Heammawihio,* The Wise One Above. *Wihio* means spider. "The spider spins a web, and goes up and down, seemingly walking on nothing" (Grinnell 1923:II, 89). *Wihio* as a stem "appears to embody the idea of mental ability of an order higher than common-superior intelligence." *Heammawihio* is the supreme deity because he knows more about how to do things than do all other creatures. Long ago, he left the earth and retired to the sky. The sun is believed to represent *Heammawihio,* although the deity is a good deal more than the sun; he is an abstraction, not just a super-brilliant, heat-radiating celestial sphere. The first offering of the pipe is made to him in all smoking.

The Earth is metaphysically conceived as having its spiritual essence in a subterranean spirit being, *Aktunowihio,* The Wise One Below, a diluted conceptual counterpart to *Heammawihio.*

The Thunder is a great bird—*Heammawihio's* bird. He brings the summer rains, with their thunder and lightning, and he is the foe of the Horned Hairy Water Spirits, the *minio.* The *minio* sometime seize people in rivers and lakes, but in some stories at least, the Thunderbird, swiftly diving from the sky, sets them free. The *minio* are bogey-like creatures; they really do not figure greatly in Cheyenne affairs, but the idea of possible contact with them frightens the more credulous Cheyennes.

Ghosts make the Cheyenne uneasy. Ghosts, or *mistai,* are spirits derived from the dead, but they are not the ghosts of particular people. The *mistai* are really poltergeists. They make their presence known by whistling and making weird noises; in very dark places, especially in the woods, they tug at one's robe; they tap and scratch on lodge coverings. In other words, they are the night noises and sensations that make even the most skeptical of us a bit jumpy when alone in the house at night or walking alone down a dark street or lane.

The soul of a person is far different. It is his *tasoom,* his shadow or shade, the vital substance and spiritual essence of the body. When it leaves the body for any length of time, death comes. Death is not personified as a being. It is simply the state of existence after the *tasoom* has separated from the body. The *tasoom* travels to the home of *Heammawihio* by way of the Milky Way, known to the Cheyennes as *ekutsihimmiyo,* The Hanging Road, which is suspended from Heaven to Earth. All the Cheyennes of the past live in heaven, just as they did on earth—and have a good time of it. As happens among many other American Indians, occasional Cheyennes who are close to death fall into a coma during which they later believe themselves to have visited the villages of those who are really dead. They are "sent back to earth" by the spirit people, and recover with vivid impressions of their experience.

For the Cheyenne there is no Hell or punishment of any sort in after-life; no Judgment or Damnation. Although Cheyennes sin when they commit murder and they often do wrong, murder is expiated in the here and now, and wrongdoing builds up no burden of guilt to be borne beyond the grave. For the Cheyenne there is no problem of salvation; goodness is to be sought as rightness for its own sake and for the appreciative approval of one's fellow man. When at last it shakes free of its corporal abode, the Cheyenne soul wafts free and light up the Hanging Road to dwell thereafter in benign proximity to the Great Wise One and the long-lost loved ones. Only the souls of those who have committed suicide are barred from this peace.

In spite of the happy destination that awaits the dead, death is clearly a traumatic experience for the surviving relatives. Each individual is highly valued, for the population is small, and every loss is keenly felt. This is why revenge drives are so strong against enemies who kill Cheyennes.

The corpse of one who has died in camp is quickly disposed of, for people feel that its ghost will not start its journey to the Milky Way until the body has been removed to its final resting place. In other words, the spirit does not take leave of the tribe until the final act of physical separation is complete. It is believed, further, that ghosts like company on their journey and that some of them try to take the spirit of a living person with them, and, hence, if the body is not disposed of with alacrity, someone may die. Children are especially susceptible to this danger.

Cheyenne burials are bundle burials. Relatives and close friends dress the body of the deceased in its finest clothing. They wrap it, extended full length with the arms at the sides, in a number of robes lashed round about with great lengths of ropes. The burial bundle is transported by travois (a vehicle made of two trailing poles supporting a platform) to its place of deposit some distance from the camp. It may be placed either in the crotch of a tree or upon a scaffold. Or it may be covered over with rocks on the ground. The owner's favorite horses are shot and left at the grave along with his weapons, or, in the case of a woman, her utensils. A man's shield and war bonnet are usually left to his son or best friend; a woman's flesher is left to her daughter. Everything else is given away, usually to nonrelatives who come to the survivor's lodge to mourn until everything has been disposed of, including the lodge. (See Llewellyn and Hoebel 1941:212-213 for the details of Cheyenne inheritance practices.)

The mourning customs fall most heavily on the women. Female relatives, especially mothers and wives, cut off their long hair and gash their foreheads so that the blood flows. If the dead one has been killed by enemies, they slash their legs so that they become caked with dried blood; sometimes the blood is not washed off for many weeks. Widows who wish to make an extravagant display of their bereavement gash themselves fearfully and move off alone to live destitute in the brush. The isolation may last a full year, until relatives begin gradually to camp around her, slowly reincorporating her into kin and community life. In these instances the death of a husband means the almost total severance of social bonds for the survivor. Mourning provides the women with their own masochistic outlet, and it may be this fact along with a feeling of loss that induces their display.

One effect of such mourning is to force the warriors to take pity on the bereaved by organizing a revenge expedition to take a scalp from the enemy tribe that did the killing. The fact that men simply let down their hair in mourning and do not lacerate or isolate themselves reveals that the death of a woman is not felt to be as deep a loss to society as is that of a man; women, in short, are not valued as highly as men. In either case, relatives exhibit their sense of loss for many years; whenever they pass the grave, they keen and wail.

Cheyenne healing rests on two different sets of medical practices. The first takes the form of empirical pharmaceutics and surgery. The second expresses itself in the form of therapeutic thaumaturgy, or curing magic, based upon a specific theory of disease causation.

Either through their own experimentation or by borrowing from others, the Cheyenne have come to possess knowledge of some fifty wild plants that have specific properties for the cure or relief of one malaise or another. They constitute remedies for headache, dizziness, constipation and diarrhea, upset stomach, vomiting, kidney trouble, hemorrhage of the lungs and bowels, nosebleed, pus-filled abscesses, poison ivy, snake bite, fever, coughs and colds, sprains and swellings, insufficient lactation, excessive menstrual bleeding, rheumatic pains, paralysis, sore gums, toothache, earache, numbness, and skin irritation; others are tranquilizers and mild, general stimulants. (See Grinnell 1923: II, 169-191 for a detailed identification of Cheyenne medicines.) The medications for these ailments are in the nature of "household" remedies. Some of them are very effective, indeed; all of them are effective to some degree. The Cheyennes know just what part of the plant is to be used in each instance. For internal cures they make effusions in the form of tea. For external applications they make either powders or poultices to be applied directly to the affected part. They have no theory as to what causes the ailments listed above; they just happen. They have no theory as to why particular herbs cure these same diseases; they just do.

In ordinary diseases herbal remedies are the first line of defense. Almost every extended family has some members who know how to prepare and administer most of the drugs known to the Cheyennes. It is the protracted and serious illness, the severe injury that calls for the work of the specialist—the medicine man and his wife. Here we move into theoretical medicine and supernaturalism. The basic Cheyenne assumption concerning serious illness is that it is caused, the causal factor being the intrusion of a tangible foreign object into the body of the person. The object may be one of a number of things: a little ball of hair, a small feather, a bit of crystal, or a thorn. The cure is performance of a ritual mumbo jumbo to locate and dislodge the element, followed by the doctor's sucking on the spot. This results in removal of the object, which is then shown by the doctor to all those in the lodge. Obviously, the effectiveness of such cures lies in their psychological influence upon the patient and his family. The mystic healing rites are nothing but intensive faith cures consisting of some crude and primitive psychosomatic therapy, reinforced with sleight-of-hand artistry on the part of the doctor. R. H. Lowie pointed out some time ago that this theoretical assumption (major diseases are things that get into the body and do violence to it in some way) and its accompanying therapeutic conclusion (these things must be gotten out of the body) are distributed among all the tribes east of the Rockies; opposite to this concept is the soul-loss theory of disease—that is, illness is caused by the capturing of the soul by a sorcerer—which predominates west of the Rockies and over into Asia (Lowie 1924:176-180).

Doctors usually purchase their curing rites from older doctors. Sometimes they get them directly in dreams—which simply means that they have watched doctors at work, learned their techniques, subconsciously assimilated them, and then bestowed upon themselves the right to use them by having a supernatural being (animal or bird or anthropomorphic figure) instruct them in dreams or visions.

When practicing, each Cheyenne doctor must be assisted by his wife or some other woman, as are the Pledgers of the major ceremonies.

Not all the work of the Cheyenne healers rests on the intrusion theory. Some of these men are skilled practitioners in dealing with bloody wounds and broken bones by use of direct surgery. These are situations in which a direct mechanical cause is easy to discern; direct, empirically arrived-at techniques are used in response. With effective technical skill, the Cheyennes have no need to fall back on a mystical theoretical concept. They can set even badly broken bones in a rawhide cast and effect totally successful fusions. They can cut out imbedded arrowheads and with astringent drugs stop the bleeding and reduce inflammation. In a few rare instances, however, they are believed to have saved lives by the concentrated use of mystic powers without either sucking or surgery. No explanation is given as to how such cures are brought about other than that birds and animals appear on the scene to work their miraculous effect.

Tabu limits Cheyenne behavior at many points of daily life. The Cheyenne assumption is that just as the prescribed acts of ritual work positively to help the universe function as desired, certain other acts work against the proper functioning of the universe. These acts (with the one exception of murder) are not generally offensive to the spirits; rather, they run contrary to the proper order of things. The violation of tabus does not bring punishment, but bad luck: life does not go according to plan and what one wishes to avoid is sure to happen. Such malfunction is the negative expression of the mechanical nature of the universe.

9

Personality and Culture

ESERVED AND DIGNIFIED, the adult Cheyenne male moves with a quiet
sense of self-assurance. He speaks fluently, but never carelessly. He is
careful of the sensibilities of others and is kindly and generous. He is
slow to anger and strives to suppress his feelings, if aggravated. Vigorous on
the hunt and in war, he prizes the active life. Towards enemies he feels no
merciful compunctions, and the more aggressive he is, the better. He is well
versed in ritual knowledge. He is neither flighty nor dour. Usually quiet, he
has a lightly displayed sense of humor. He is sexually repressed and masochistic, but that masochism is expressed in culturally approved rites. He does
not show much creative imagination in artistic expression, but he has a firm
grip on reality. He deals with the problems of life in set ways while at the
same time showing a notable capacity to readjust to new circumstances. His
thinking is rationalistic to a high degree and yet colored with mysticism. His
ego is strong and not easily threatened. His superego, as manifest in his strong
social conscience and mastery of his basic impulses, is powerful and dominating.
He is "mature"—serene and composed, secure in his social position, capable
of warm social relations. He has powerful anxieties, but these are channeled
into institutionalized modes of collective expression with satisfactory results.
He exhibits few neurotic tendencies.

The typical grown-up Cheyenne woman exhibits much the same con-
stellation of traits. Not having the direct outlet for aggressive impulses that
men find in war, she is touchier in domestic relations and apt to be a bit willful
within her family. Grinnell calls her "masterful." She is more artistically creative than the male, but still within prescribed limits. She is equally repressed
sexually but manifests less compensatory behavior in masochism and aggression
against enemies—although both these traits are discernible in her.

The molding of the adult, of course, begins in infancy. Cheyenne children are highly valued by their parents and by the tribe. From the outset,
their lives are made as comfortable as is possible. They are strictly taught and

steadily but gently molded toward the Cheyenne ideal in an atmosphere of love and interest. The Cheyenne child is rarely physically punished, and we have seen how daughters may react in suicide if their mothers are overly harsh or vindictive after they have grown up.

Birth is attended to by the female relatives of the mother assisted by some knowledgeable old midwives. A special birth lodge is sometimes raised, although most births take place in the home tipi. The mother in labor does not lie in bed but kneels on a hay-covered robe before a stout frame of poles set firmly in the ground. She seizes a vertical pole and is embraced from the front by a midwife, who braces her own back against the framework. Another midwife receives the baby and removes it from the rear.

As soon as the baby is born, the mother's uvula is tickled to make her gag, thus forcing out the placenta, which is wrapped in a bundle and hung out in a tree. The baby's umbilical cord is cut, tied, and salved. When it finally drops off, it is carefully saved by the mother, dried, and sewed into a little buckskin bag to be kept by the child until he grows up, perhaps well into adulthood. According to the Cheyenne, the navel contains some of the essence of a child's personality, and the child who does not care for his umbilical will be disobedient and bad. Except for this belief, there is little of the mystical in Cheyenne birth practices. Mothers, it is true, must observe a few minor prenatal tabus, and a medicine man may be engaged to sing during the birth, but the general tenor of the whole proceeding is one of practical obstetrics. The father may not enter the tipi until after the baby is born; but he is busy with practical tasks outside, keeping the fire going and helping the woman who is cooking a meal for the birth attendants. He engages in no magic, observes no special tabus, nor engages in anything resembling the couvade. Nor is the mother ritually isolated after giving birth. She rests in the tipi for four days, it is true, and during this time her child is wet-nursed, but the idea behind this practice is that she needs rest to regain her strength. There are no purificatory rites before she or her baby may rejoin the society.

Newborn babies are gently greased, powdered, and wrapped in soft robes. If the weather is cold, they are carried in the mother's arms for warmth and comfort. Cheyenne mothers use the cradleboard—a wooden frame carried on the mother's back and on which is a laced-up animal-skin "cocoon" in which the infant is tightly bound like a mummy. The baby is ordinarily not put on the cradleboard until some weeks after its birth. The advantage of its use is that the mother may go about her work with an assurance that her baby will not get into trouble. If traveling, or watching a dance or ceremony, she carries the board like a knapsack; when working in the lodge, she hangs it upright from one of the lodge poles; when working outside the lodge, she leans it against the lodge covering. Although the infant is tightly confined when tied in the cradleboard, this does not retard its development in learning to walk or in other phases of growth. It must early learn quiet patience, however. Crying is not tolerated. The Cheyennes say this is because a squalling baby might give away the camp position at night when enemy raiders are seeking it for an attack. On a deeper level, however, the Cheyennes abhor anyone forcing his will upon others by self-display, and this behavior principle must be learned from the outset. Crying babies are not scolded, slapped, or threatened. They are simply taken out on the cradleboard away from the camp and into the brush where they are hung on a bush. There the squalling infant is left alone until it cries itself out. A few such experiences indelibly teach it that bawling brings not reward but complete and total rejection and the loss of all social contacts. On the other hand, the good baby is cuddled and constantly loved. When not on the board it is rocked in the arms of its mother or grandmother and soothed with lullabies. It is nursed whenever it shows a desire (self-demand feeding).

As the infant gets a little older, it is more often carried about on its mother's back in a blanket sling rather than on the cradleboard. Its head projects about her shoulders; it hears and sees all she does; it shares the warmth of her body and feels the movements of her muscles; it receives food passed over the mother's shoulder; it even sleeps on her back as she goes about her household tasks. It is enveloped in warmth, movement, and affectionate attention. Its body is gently soothed with medicated ointments and soft vegetable ointments. Its early years are full of adult-given gratification. Its frustrations must, however, be quickly internalized, for the alternative is isolation in the brush. This is the first lesson learned, and it must be remembered at all times; it pervades Cheyenne life. Children are to be quiet and respectful in the presence of elders. The learned have much to offer, and what one acquires in wisdom about the Cheyenne way one acquires through learning taught by those who know the way. Cheyenne relations between younger and elder are thus the relations of pupils and teachers—and pupils must be deferential.

On the basis of this well-established relationship, Cheyenne children are continuously exhorted by their elders: "Be brave, be honest, be virtuous, be industrious, be generous, do not quarrel! If you do not do these things, people will talk about you in the camp; they will not respect you; you will be shamed. If you listen to this advice you will grow up to be a good man or woman, and you will amount to something." The values of the Cheyennes are made explicit in a steady stream of sermonizing that expostulates what is deeply woven into everyday life. The values are reinforced by many explicit mechanisms of public and family approval.

A child does not have to wait until he is grown up to be able to practice what is preached and to experience the satisfaction of performance. Cheyenne children are little replicas of their elders in interests and deed. Children begin to learn adult activities and practice them in play at incredibly early ages. Boys learn to ride almost as soon as they learn to walk, girls soon after. At two or three, they ride with their mothers, and by the time they are five or six, little boys are riding bareback on their own colts and mastering the use of the lasso. By seven or eight, they help with the herding of the camp's horses. Little girls, as soon as they can toddle, follow their mothers to gather wood and bring in water, the mothers patiently helping them with their pint-sized burdens. Boys get small, but good quality, bows and arrows as soon as they can effectively learn to use them. As Grinnell observed,

In their hunting, these tiny urchins displayed immense caution and patience, creeping stealthily about through the underbush of the river bottom,
or among the sagebrush on the prairie. . . . The care with which they
twisted and wound in and out of cover when approaching the game, taking
advantage of every inequality in the ground, of the brush, and of the
clumps of ryegrass, was precisely what they would have to practice when
hunting in later life. (Grinnell 1923:I:115)

Until they are twelve or thirteen, when they are ready for real hunting
and their first war expeditions, the boys join with the girls at "play camp."
The girls have small tipis, made for them by their mothers. The boys choose
older girls to be their mothers; the smallest children are used as babies, and
the routine of full family life is mimicked throughout the day. The boys catch
fish and bring in birds and rabbits for their food. They cannot kill real buffalo,
but they have great fun with imitation buffalo surrounds. The boys who are
the make-believe buffalo carry a prickly pear on a stick to represent the buffalo's
horns and heart. They go out first to "graze." Other boys, mounted on sticks,
ride out to surround them and charge in with their bows and blunt arrows
for the "kill." An arrow in the center of the prickly pear brings down the
game; if it is off the center, the "bull" is only wounded and turns and charges
to give the unskilled hunter a swat on his rear end with the spiny cactus. War
is also played with faithful mimicry of the real thing, including the dismantling
of the "camp" by the girls, who flee to safety with their "children" and be-
longings while their "men" try to stave off the enemy. In the play associated
with the children's camps (which, incidentally, they call "large play" in contrast to small girls' and boys' play with dolls and toy bows and arrows, which
is called "small play") they even put on Sun Dances. Some of the boys may
pierce themselves with cactus thorns and drag chunks of wood, calling them
buffalo skulls.

A boy's first real hunt and war party comes early in life—at twelve or
thirteen. His first buffalo kill is rewarded with great public recognition, if his
family can afford it. His father calls out the news for all in the camp to hear,
and he announces that he is giving a good horse—even his best one—to some
poor man, in honor of the event. This man gets on the horse to ride all around
the camp, singing a song in praise of the boy. The youngster's mother may
get up a feast, to which the father publicly invites a number of poor people
to share in the family's good fortune. Gifts of blankets and other valuables
may be distributed at the end of the feast. The same thing is done when a boy
comes home from his first war party.

It is easy to imagine the sense of glowing pride of the young teen-ager
who gets such attention on his first manly successes. Cheyenne youths have
little reason to be rebels-without-cause. They slip early into manhood, knowing
their contributions are immediately wanted, valued, and ostentatiously rewarded. In the family response we see also the signalizing of Cheyenne social
consciousness. Some families do better than others, winning more goods and
more prestige, but what they have is shared with those who are less able and
more luckless. The boy and his parents get tremendous ego-gratification; at

the same time, however, they must think of others. Here, too, we see revealed the Cheyenne attitude toward wealth. It is not to be hoarded or to be self-consumed. Stinginess and miserliness are un-Cheyenne. Its value derives from its being given away. Chiefs, who are the greatest exemplars of Cheyenne virtues, are the greatest givers. Note also, that the Cheyennes do not expect an equal return in gifts, except in marriage exchanges; nor is there anything comparable to the Northwest Coast Indian potlatch with its competitive rivalries. Cheyenne boys learn to become highly competitive in the skills of hunt and war. They are rewarded with great individual prestige for successful performance, but the fact is also impressed upon them that they fight for the benefit of the tribe, "to protect the people," and that the fruits of the hunt are to be widely shared.

It is also important to observe that there are no initiation or puberty rites for boys in Cheyenne culture. Cheyenne children acquire full adult status by performance, without the necessity of undergoing hazing by the old men or any other form of *rite de passage*. This fact is illustrated in the timing of the piercing of the ears (pierced ears hold the rings with which the Cheyennes are so fond of adorning themselves). In many parts of the world this event would be part of the puberty ceremonies, and the privilege of wearing the decorations would be an indication of adult status. Not so, with the Cheyennes: ears are ceremonially pierced at the ages of three to six, the action being performed on occasion of the tribal ceremonial gatherings. The honored man who is to pierce a child's ears is sent for by the father through the medium of a crier, who makes the announcement to all the camp. The ear piercer counts coup, performs his task, and receives a munificent present of horses or other goods.

One might say that if there is any initiation for the Cheyenne boy, it takes place on his first warpath.

> . . . in all ways the journey was made easy for them. Yet when the moment came to fight, they were given every opportunity to distinguish themselves. . . . While such little boys did not often accomplish any great feat, yet sometimes they did so, and returned to the village covered with glory, to the unspeakable delight and pride of their families, and to be objects of respect and admiration to their less ambitious and energetic playfellows. (Grinnell 1923:I, 122-123)

Such a boy receives a new name, chosen from among those belonging to his family's most outstanding predecessors. He is now, indeed, a full-fledged adult.

For the Cheyenne girl, on the other hand, there is a clear-cut transition rite. Before the time of her menses, however, she, like the boy, receives continuous encouragement and family rewards for her achievements. My own Cheyenne informant, Calf Woman, was seven when her mother started her on her first robe quilling. When she had finished it and placed it over her little baby niece as a present, her grown-up brother said, "Well, I shall have to give her a present to keep her up. She will learn to expect things for her efforts." And he gave her a pony. Later, when a baby girl was born to her brother, Calf Woman beaded a cradleboard for the infant. Her brother gave her a mare.

The first menstruation of a girl is a great event. She has entered woman-hood, and her father calls the news to the entire camp from beside his lodge door. If wealthy in horses, he gives one away to signalize the occasion. Like other Indians, the Cheyennes nonetheless consider menstrual blood to be defiling and inimical to the virility of males and to their supernatural powers. The girl therefore retires to an isolation, or moon, hut so that there will be no danger of her polluting her father's or brothers' sacred paraphernalia. Before going, however, she lets down her hair, bathes, and has her body painted all over in red by her older woman relatives. She takes a ceremonial incense puri-fication just before she goes into the hut, where she remains four days with her grandmother, who looks after her and advises her on womanly conduct. At the end of the period, she is again smudged completely to purify her for reentry into social life. Until menarche, all Cheyenne women leave their tipis for the moon lodge, but only unmarried girls must go through the purification each time.

After her first menses, each girl receives her chastity belt from her mother. She wears it constantly until married. Even after marriage she wears it whenever her husband is away at war or on the hunt. She wears it whenever she goes away from her lodge to gather wood or water. For any man other than her husband to touch it is a private delict of the first magnitude. In one case, a man was nearly stoned to death by the girl and her mother in a surprise ambush. The least that the miscreant may expect is that the girl's female rela-tives will charge his camp and destroy it. In the one case in which this actually happened, the parents of the guilty boy made no resistance.

Individual assaults with intent to rape are nonexistent among the Chey-enne—except for the case of Bear Rope, who assaulted his daughter. She dis-emboweled him with a knife while protecting her virtue. The Arrows were renewed for Bear Rope's death, but the daughter was not exiled, for her parricide was justified.

The sexual repression and self-control of the Cheyennes have been suf-ficiently noted in our previous discussions. Its harmless aggressive outlet in the men's attacks on the root diggers has been described. Its masochistic ex-pression in the self-aggression of Sun Dance torture and self-sacrifice of flesh and fingers has been detailed. In only one institutionalized practice within the tribe are the floodgates opened to release all the pent-up, subconscious, frus-tration-bred sexual aggression of the males. This is supposed to take place when a woman is flagrantly adulterous. In the four cases which we were able to record (Llewellyn and Hoebel 1941:202-210) the triggering events were desertion, simple adultery, and refusal to enter into a sororate marriage—all exasperating actions by strong-willed women toward men who claimed a hus-band's rights. The response is to "put a woman on the prairie," called *noha'sȝwȝstan* (literally "any man's wife"). The outraged husband invites all the unmarried members of his military society (excepting his wife's relatives) to a feast on the prairie. There the woman is raped by each of them in turn. Big Footed Woman was forced into intercourse with forty or more of her husband's confreres when a young wife. She survived it and lived to be a hundred, but no one ever married her afterwards. Tassel Woman was nearly dead when she was rescued by Blue Wing and his wife. The right of a husband to give his wife to his soldier "brothers" is not denied, yet it is a formal right that the Cheyennes in fact cannot accept with equanimity. In two cases, the brothers and father of the woman went forth to attack the whole soldier band, threatening to shoot to kill regardless of the ban on murder. The soldiers scattered and kept out of their way. In the case of Little Sea Shell, the girl fled to the wife of the Keeper of the Holy Hat, for the band was on the march and the Hat Keeper's wife had the Buffalo Hat Bundle on her back at the time. The lodge of the Hat Keeper is an asylum in which even an enemy raider may find sanctuary. If he can get to the Holy Hat Lodge, he is immune and will be escorted safely out of Cheyenne country. In this instance, the Hat Keeper's wife made a symbolic lodge by putting her arms about Little Sea Shell while holding a stick associated with the Hat Bundle. Her quick thinking saved the girl.

Men who have participated in a gang rape are not proud of it. The women in the camps taunt them, and they do not defend themselves; they just hang their heads and walk away. Clearly, the deed runs counter to dominant Cheyenne values. We suspect that the right of the husband to do this to his wife is very old and may have some sacred significance. Grinnell mentions that just before the great fight with the Pawnees and Potawatomi, in 1853, Long Chin was putting on the Holy Hat to wear in the battle when the chin strap broke. This was very bad luck, so to counteract it Long Chin "publicly pledged himself to give a woman to be passed on the prairie" (Grinnell 1915: 88). The deed may originally have had some of the quality of the action in which the wife of a Pledger of one of the great ceremonies is offered to the High Priest or Instructor. In any event, the practice is an anomaly in terms of Cheyenne ideals, but understandable in terms of psychodynamics.

According to formal belief, any woman who has been four times divorced becomes a "free woman"—any man's game. Although there is no memory of this ever having happened, one of the four Virgins of the Elk Soldiers was once put on this footing because she had lost her virginity before marriage. The Elks cut her hair and turned her loose, publicly disgraced. No man would marry her, although many went to her for intercourse. She was really a kind of outlaw—like the banished Sticks-Everything-Under-His-Belt. But, like him, she was rehabilitated and reinstated in the tribe by a Sun Dance pledged in her honor, sometime around 1865. In the Sun Dance, the priest prayed to Maiyun to give her a new life, and when it was over, the Pledger married her. Like the earth, she was renewed, and she lived faultlessly with her husband for many years.

Finally, the inversion of Cheyenne personality in the Contraries needs to be examined in the present context. It will be remembered that a small handful of men reject the male warrior role by becoming transvestites. Others, the Contraries, overdo the warrior role in an institutionalized form of pathological exaggeration. The first important fact is that the Contraries may not marry. If they do, they must give up their lances and behave like normal people.

The second fact is that the Contraries court death with extreme recklessness in battle; their lances give them "great luck," however, and they are hard to kill. We put these two facts together and suggest the following: the Contraries, like the Halfmen-halfwomen, are neurotically anxious about sex relations and their own virility. Whereas, the Halfmen-halfwomen find their refuge in total rejection of male sexuality, the Contraries seek validation in an exaggerated male rejection of heterosexuality.

The symbol of the Contrary is the Thunder Bow, a special bow decorated with magic feathers and bearing a lancehead on one end. An ordinary lance is a perfectly good weapon that may or may not be endowed with sexual symbolism. The Thunder Bow is not a weapon, however. It is carried in battle, but it is used only to count coup. It is significant that its point may not touch the earth—the bearer of life, the essence of femininity. Symbolically, the Thunder Bow suggests the male sex organ tied and restrained.

Two further facts that demonstrate the sexual implications of this status are, first, that a Contrary may never sit or lie upon a bed and, second, that a man becomes a Contrary because "he is afraid of thunder and lightning." He dreams that he must become a Contrary and that this will cure him of his anxiety. The Thunder-bird, from whom the Contraries' great supernatural power comes, is a male figure.

In his rejection of heterosexuality, the Contrary rejects normal social relations. He must live alone, apart from all the camp. Whatever he does in social relations he does backwards. Ask him to do one thing and he will do its opposite. Even in battle, he cannot charge with the other warriors at his side, or in front or behind him. He must be off on the flanks, alone. When he holds his Thunder Bow in his right hand, he may not retreat.

The Contrary, then, is the Cheyenne warrior male with a monomania for what might be called military virility. For this, he is highly respected—and pitied. The Cheyennes say it is a fearsome and difficult thing to be a Contrary, an almost unbearable burden. Contrariness may be seen as providing a customary outlet through which extreme cases of anxiety are turned constructively to the social benefit of a warrior nation. Yet, if it were allowed to spread throughout the society, it would rend the social fabric. This threat is mastered by limiting the number of Contraries to two or three. A man may become a Contrary only by purchasing the Thunder Bow and power of one who is already a Contrary. The seller is then released of his obligations and may marry and return to normal life.

In summing up this study of the Cheyennes, the following points must be mentioned. The Cheyennes stand out among the nomadic Indians of the Plains for their dignity, chastity, steadfast courage, and tightly structured, yet flexible, social organization. Never a large tribe, they have held their own with outstanding success. They have come to terms with their environment and with themselves. They are exceedingly rational and skilled in cultural adaptation through felicitous social inventiveness and manipulation. Although deep down they are beset with anxieties, their anxieties are institutionally controlled.

Their adaptation to the Plains way of life was sudden and rapid. In this situation of flux they have faced three great threats: famine, enemies, and internal disruption. They ward off famine with carefully police-controlled group hunting, abetted by occasional supernaturally directed group hunts, and they constantly reassure themselves by tribal World Renewal ceremonies. They hold off their enemies by exaltation of the military life combined with a system of firm alliances with selected neighboring tribes. They counter the forces of internal disruption (in part engendered by the training and values necessary to successful war making) by repression of sex, by vesting authority in those who are learned, by organized government and removal of tribal chiefs from status competition, by emphasis on altruism, by banishment of murderers, and by reinforcement of tribal unity through the great tribal ceremonies. Reasonably effective mechanisms for intrasocietal release of aggressive tensions are provided in mock battles between men and women, in a variety of competitive games, in self-torture, and in institutionalized role transfers for a few of the men.

The major basic postulates underlying Cheyenne culture, and therefore dominant in the control of Cheyenne behavior, are as follows:

POSTULATE I. The world (universe) is fundamentally a mechanical system with a limited energy quotient which progressively diminishes as it is expended.

POSTULATE II. The energy quotient of the world is rechargeable through compulsive mimetic acts of sympathetic ritual.

Corollary 1. Ritual officiants must learn the exact formulas of world renewal from knowledgable experts.

Corollary 2. Acts are more effective than words.

POSTULATE III. Man is subordinate to supernatural forces and spirit beings. These forces and beings have superior knowledge concerning the operation of the universe and are benevolently inclined toward man.

Corollary 1. Tribal well-being and individual success are abetted by the tutelage or blessing of the supernaturals.

Corollary 2. Prayer, pledges, and self-sacrifice win the attention and help of the supernaturals.

POSTULATE IV. The social order is fragile and threatened by aggressive tendencies in Cheyenne character.

Corollary 1. All first obligations are to the maintenance of the well-being of the tribe.

Corollary 2. All aggressive behavior within the tribe is dangerous and bad.

POSTULATE V. The authority of the tribal council is derived from the supernaturals and is supreme over all other elements in the society.

POSTULATE VI. The killing of a Cheyenne by a Cheyenne pollutes the tribal fetishes and the murderer.

Corollary 1. Bad luck will dog the tribe until the fetishes are purified.

Corollary 2. Murderers may not be killed but must be separated from the social body through banishment.

POSTULATE VII. Sex interests generate jealousy and hostility; they must be held to a minimum.

Corollary 1. Chastity and abstinence are good.

Corollary 2. Marriage among relatives is impossible.

POSTULATE VIII. Sex relations are necessary for procreation and regenerative ritual.

Corollary 1. Women must officially participate in religious rituals and in curing.

POSTULATE IX. War is necessary to defend and advance the interests of the tribe.

POSTULATE X. War is necessary to permit individual self-expression and personality development of the male:

POSTULATE XI. The virility of men, like the energy of the world, is limited.

Corollary 1. Male genitals must be magically protected.

Corollary 2. Abstinence conserves male energy for war.

POSTULATE XII. Men are more important than women.

Corollary 1. The husband is the head of the household.

Corollary 2. All governmental posts are held by men.

POSTULATE XIII. Children (excluding infants) have the same qualities as adults; they lack only in experience.

Corollary 1. Children should, on their level, engage in adult activities.

Corollary 2. Children become adults as soon as they are physically able to perform adult roles.

POSTULATE XIV. All land, and the tribal fetishes, are public property.

POSTULATE XV. All other material goods are private property, but they should be generously shared with others.

POSTULATE XVI. The individual personality is important.

Corollary 1. The individual must be permitted and encouraged to express his potentiality with the greatest possible freedom compatible with group existence.

Corollary 2. Rehabilitation of delinquents and criminals after punishment is extremely important.

These principles form the bedrock upon which the Cheyennes have raised their cultural edifice, which is for them The Cheyenne Way.

Bibliography

ANDERSON, R., 1956, The Buffalo Men, A Cheyenne Ceremony of Petition Deriving from the Sutaio. *Southwestern Journal of Anthropology*, Vol. 12, 92-104.

BENNETT, J. W., 1944, The Development of Ethnological Theories as Illustrated by the Plains Indian Sun Dance. *American Anthropologist*, Vol. 46, 162-181.

DORSEY, G. A., 1905, The Cheyenne. Field Columbian Museum, *Anthropological Series*, Vol. IX, Nos. 1 and 2.

EASTMAN, E. G., 1935, *Pratt: the Red Man's Moses*. Norman, Okla.: University of Oklahoma Press.

EGGAN, F., 1955, The Cheyenne and Arapaho Kinship System. In *Social Anthropology of North American Tribes* (enlarged edition). Chicago: University of Chicago Press, pp. 35-95.

FORTUNE, R. F., 1932, *Sorcerers of Dobu: The Social Anthropology of the Dobu Islanders of the Western Pacific*. New York: Dutton.

GLADWIN, T., 1957, Personality Structure in the Plains. *Anthropological Quarterly*, Vol. 30, 111-124.

GRINNELL, G. B., 1915, *The Fighting Cheyennes*. New York: Scribner.

———, 1923, *The Cheyenne Indians: Their History and Ways of Life* (2 vols.). New Haven: Yale University Press.

HILGER, M. I., 1946, Notes on Cheyenne Child Life. *American Anthropologist*, Vol. 48, 60-69.

HOEBEL, E. A., N.d., Cheyenne field notes. Unpublished.

KLUCKHOHN, C., 1949, The Philosophy of the Navaho Indians. In F. S. C. Northrop (ed.), *Ideological Differences and World Order*. New Haven: Yale University Press.

LAVENDER, D., 1954, *Bent's Fort*. New York: Doubleday.

LLEWELLYN, K. N., and E. A. Hoebel, 1941, *The Cheyenne Way: Conflict and Case Law in Primitive Jurisprudence*. Norman, Okla.: University of Oklahoma Press.

LOWIE, R. H., 1916, Plains Indian Age Societies. American Museum of Natural History, *Anthropological Papers*, Vol. 11, 877-992.

————, 1924, *Primitive Religion*. New York: Boni and Liveright.

————, 1935, *The Crow Indians*. New York: Farrar and Rinehart.

MICHELSON, T., 1932, The Narrative of a Southern Cheyenne Woman. *Smithsonian Miscellaneous Collections*, Vol. 87, No. 5.

MOONEY, J., 1907, The Cheyenne Indians. American Anthropological Association, *Memoirs*, Vol. 1, Part 6.

PETTER, R. C., 1907, Sketch of the Cheyenne Grammar. American Anthropological Association, *Memoirs*, Vol. 1, Part 6.

————, 1915, *English-Cheyenne Dictionary*. Kettle Falls, Washington.

————, 1952, *Cheyenne Grammar*. Newton, Kans.: Menonite Publication Office.

PETTITT, G. A., 1946, Primitive Education in North America. *University of California Publications in American Archaeology and Ethnology*, Vol. 43, No. 1.

SPIER, L., 1921, The Plains Indian Sun Dance. American Museum of Natural History, *Anthropological Papers*, Vol. 16, Part 7.

TYLOR, E. B., 1889, On a Method of Investigating the Development of Institutions: Applied to the Laws of Marriage and Descent. *Journal of the Royal Anthropological Institute of Great Britain and Ireland*, Vol. 18, 245-272.

UNDERHILL, R. M., 1948, Ceremonial Patterns in the Greater Southwest. New York: American Ethnological Society, Monograph XII.

WARD, R. D., 1925, *The Climates of the United States*. Boston: Ginn.

WEBB, W. P., 1931, *The Great Plains*. Boston: Ginn.

WILSON, G. R., 1934, The Hidatsa Earth-lodge. American Museum of Natural History, *Anthropological Papers*, Vol. 33.

Recommended Reading

on the Cheyenne and Other Plains Indians

BOWERS, A. W., 1950, *Mandan Social and Ceremonial Organization*. Chicago: University of Chicago Press.

Includes a summary of Mandan social organization, plus detailed descriptions of the major Mandan ceremonials.

EWERS, J. C., 1939, *Plains Indian Painting: A Description of Aboriginal American Art*. Stanford, Calif.: Stanford University Press.

Illustrates and analyzes the patterns of painting on hides throughout the Plains.

GRINNELL, G. B., 1915, *The Fighting Cheyennes*. New York: Scribner.

Gripping accounts of all the Cheyenne battles from 1837 to 1879 as told to Grinnell by the Cheyennes themselves.

————, 1923, *The Cheyenne Indians: Their History and Way of Life* (2 vols.). New Haven: Yale University Press.

Covers most aspects of Cheyenne culture in a detailed, descriptive manner without interpretive analysis.

JABLOW, J., n.d., The Cheyenne in Plains Indian Trade Relations 1795-1840. *American Ethnological Society*, Memoir 19.

A scholarly treatment of historical sources that throws light on early relations of the Cheyennes to white traders and neighboring tribes.

LLEWELLYN, K. N., and E. A. HOEBEL, 1941, *The Cheyenne Way: Conflict and Case Law in Primitive Jurisprudence*. Norman, Okla.: University of Oklahoma Press.

Presents many descriptive accounts of intratribal disputes and how they were handled.

Lowie, R. H., 1935, *The Crow Indians*. New York: Farrar and Rinehart. Emphasizes the Crow view of life, as well as their way of life.

―――, 1954, *Indians of the Plains*. New York: McGraw-Hill. American Museum of Natural History Hand Book Series, No. 1.

The only general book on Plains Indians. It offers a simple but authoritative comparative summary of Plains Indian culture as a whole.

Marriott, A., 1945, *The Ten Grandmothers*. Norman, Okla.: University of Oklahoma Press.

A superbly written, seminovelized account of Kiowa Indian life and history. Accurate and moving.

Sandoz, M., 1955, *Cheyenne Autumn*. New York: McGraw-Hill.

A true and insightful account of the Cheyenne trek from Indian Territory to their northern home in 1878 and the subsequent massacre at Ft. Robinson the following year.

Seagar, J. H. (S. Vestal, ed.), 1924, *Early Days Among the Cheyenne and Arapaho Indians*. Norman, Okla.: University of Oklahoma Press.

A simple and straightforward story of the Cheyennes in the early reservation days, told by a brave and understanding agency employee.

Smith, M. W., 1938, The War Complex of Plains Indians. *Proceedings of the American Philosophical Society*, Vol. 78, No. 3, 425-464.

A comparative summary of war in Plains Indian culture.

Wallace, E., and E. A. Hoebel, 1952, *The Comanches: Lords of the South Plains*. Norman, Okla.: University of Oklahoma Press.

A full and vigorous account of the Cheyennes' stout allies.